DASH DIET SOLUTION
HIGH BLOOD P

TRANSFORM YOUR LIFE WITH PROVEN RECIPES AND PRACTICAL TIPS TO COMBAT HIGH BLOOD PRESSURE

Table of Contents

Introduction

The DASH diet is a scientifically-backed eating plan designed to lower blood pressure, reduce the risk of chronic conditions, and support weight loss. A DASH diet cookbook serves as a valuable resource for anyone looking to embrace this health-promoting and straightforward eating plan. Prioritizing nutrient-dense foods from all food groups is essential for maintaining optimal health. The DASH diet emphasizes a low-fat, low-sodium, and calorie-conscious approach, focusing on whole grains, fruits, vegetables, fish, and poultry.

Developed by the U.S. government as part of the Dietary Approaches to Stop Hypertension program, the DASH diet has gained widespread recognition as a practical and sustainable eating plan. A DASH diet cookbook empowers individuals to embark on this lifestyle by teaching them how to create delicious and nutritious meals.

Adhering to the DASH diet involves selecting foods high in vitamins and minerals but low in fat and sodium, such as fruits, vegetables, fish, poultry, and whole grains. At the same time, it's important to limit red meat, sugary treats, and high-fat dairy products. Beyond dietary adjustments, the DASH diet also encourages regular physical activity and stress management techniques to support overall health and wellness.

Perfect for individuals with busy lifestyles, the DASH diet and a DASH diet cookbook offer quick, easy meal options that are both healthful and flavorful. The diet is designed to facilitate the maintenance of a healthy lifestyle without compromising busy schedules. With the aid of a DASH diet cookbook, families can transition to healthier eating habits without sacrificing taste or convenience. This book will guide you through the fundamentals of the DASH diet, provide practical tips for success, and offer a collection of delicious recipes tailored for 1-2 servings, making it easy for you to embark on this life-changing journey.

1. Introduction to High Blood Pressure

What is High Blood Pressure?

High blood pressure, also known as hypertension, is a condition in which the force of blood against the walls of your arteries is consistently too high. Blood pressure is measured using two numbers: systolic pressure (the higher number) represents the pressure in your blood vessels when your heart beats, while diastolic pressure (the lower number) represents the pressure in your blood vessels when your heart is at rest between beats. A normal blood pressure reading is typically around 120/80 mm Hg.

High blood pressure is diagnosed when a person's blood pressure consistently measures at or above 130/80 mm Hg. It is essential to monitor and manage high blood pressure because if left untreated, it can lead to various health problems.

Risks and Causes of High Blood Pressure

There are several risk factors and causes associated with high blood pressure. Some of these include:

- Age: The risk of high blood pressure increases as you get older.
- Family history: If your family members have a history of hypertension, you may be at a higher risk.
- Race: Some ethnic groups, such as African Americans, are more likely to develop high blood pressure.
- Obesity: Excess weight can put more strain on your heart and blood vessels, contributing to hypertension.
- Physical inactivity: A sedentary lifestyle can lead to weight gain and increased blood pressure.
- Tobacco use: Smoking or using tobacco products can cause your blood vessels to narrow, leading to increased blood pressure.
- Excessive alcohol consumption: Drinking too much alcohol can elevate blood pressure.
- High-sodium diet: Consuming too much salt can cause your body to retain fluid, which may increase blood pressure.
- Chronic stress: Long-term stress can cause a sustained increase in blood pressure.

Consequences of High Blood Pressure

If left uncontrolled, high blood pressure can lead to various health problems, including:

Heart disease: Hypertension can increase the risk of coronary artery disease, heart attack, and heart failure.

Stroke: High blood pressure can cause blood vessels in your brain to rupture or become blocked, leading to a stroke.

Kidney damage: Hypertension can damage the blood vessels in your kidneys, impairing their function and potentially leading to kidney failure.

Vision loss: High blood pressure can damage blood vessels in your eyes, resulting in vision problems or even blindness.

Sexual dysfunction: Hypertension can cause erectile dysfunction in men and reduced libido in women.

Cognitive decline: High blood pressure can contribute to memory problems and decreased cognitive function as you age.

Understanding the risks, causes, and consequences of high blood pressure is essential for taking proactive steps towards managing it. The following chapters will introduce you to the DASH diet and other lifestyle changes that can help you lower your blood pressure and improve your overall health.

2. Understanding the DASH Diet

Overview of the DASH Diet

The DASH diet, which stands for Dietary Approaches to Stop Hypertension, is a dietary pattern designed to help lower blood pressure and improve overall cardiovascular health. The DASH diet focuses on consuming nutrient-dense foods that are rich in essential vitamins, minerals, and fiber, while limiting those high in sodium, saturated fat, and added sugars.

The primary components of the DASH diet include:

1) Fruits and vegetables: These provide essential vitamins, minerals, and fiber, which can help lower blood pressure.
2) Whole grains: Rich in fiber and nutrients, whole grains can help manage blood pressure by promoting a feeling of fullness and supporting healthy digestion.
3) Low-fat or fat-free dairy products: These provide essential nutrients like calcium, potassium, and magnesium, which play a crucial role in regulating blood pressure.
4) Lean protein sources: Fish, poultry, and plant-based proteins like legumes and nuts are encouraged, as they are lower in saturated fat compared to red meat.
5) Nuts, seeds, and healthy fats: These are nutrient-dense and can provide heart-healthy fats, which can help improve overall cardiovascular health.

History of the DASH Diet

The DASH diet was developed in the early 1990s through a series of clinical studies funded by the National Institutes of Health (NIH) and the National Heart, Lung, and Blood Institute (NHLBI). These studies aimed to identify an effective dietary pattern for reducing high blood pressure. The research revealed that the DASH diet effectively lowered blood pressure in participants, regardless of age, sex, or ethnicity.

Since its inception, the DASH diet has consistently been recognized as one of the top diets for overall health by health professionals and organizations. It has been endorsed by the American Heart Association, the American College of Cardiology, and the U.S. Department of Agriculture (USDA), among others.

Benefits of the DASH Diet

In addition to lowering blood pressure, the DASH diet offers several other health benefits, including:

6) Improved cardiovascular health: The DASH diet can reduce the risk of developing heart disease and stroke by promoting better blood pressure and cholesterol levels.
7) Weight loss and management: By emphasizing nutrient-dense, low-calorie foods and portion control, the DASH diet can support healthy weight loss and long-term weight maintenance.
8) Better blood sugar control: The high-fiber, low-sugar nature of the DASH diet can help regulate blood sugar levels, which is particularly beneficial for individuals with diabetes or prediabetes.
9) Enhanced kidney function: The DASH diet can help protect the kidneys by promoting healthy blood pressure and reducing the risk of kidney stones.
10) Reduced inflammation: The nutrient-rich, whole food-based nature of the DASH diet can help decrease inflammation throughout the body, which is associated with a lower risk of chronic diseases.

By understanding the principles, history, and benefits of the DASH diet, you can make informed decisions about how to incorporate this evidence-based dietary approach into your daily life. The following chapters will provide guidance on the foods to eat and avoid, tips for successful meal planning, and delicious recipes tailored to the DASH diet.

3. Foods to Eat and Avoid on the DASH Diet

In order to successfully implement the DASH diet, it's essential to understand which foods are encouraged and discouraged. This chapter will provide a comprehensive overview of the types of foods to eat and avoid, focusing on nutrients and food groups.

Foods to Eat on the DASH Diet

The DASH diet emphasizes nutrient-dense foods that are rich in vitamins, minerals, and fiber. Here are the key food groups and examples of foods to include in your diet:

- Fruits:
    - Fresh, frozen, or canned fruits (without added sugar)
    - Examples: apples, oranges, bananas, berries, pears, peaches, melons
- Vegetables:
    - Fresh, frozen, or canned vegetables (without added salt)
    - Examples: leafy greens, broccoli, carrots, tomatoes, bell peppers, zucchini
- Whole grains:
    - Unprocessed or minimally processed grains
    - Examples: whole wheat bread, brown rice, quinoa, oats, barley, whole grain pasta
- Lean protein sources:
    - Fish, poultry, and plant-based proteins
    - Examples: salmon, tuna, chicken, turkey, beans, lentils, tofu, tempeh
- Low-fat or fat-free dairy products:
    - Dairy products with reduced or no fat content
    - Examples: skim milk, low-fat yogurt, reduced-fat cheese
- Nuts, seeds, and healthy fats:
    - Unsaturated fats and nutrient-rich plant sources
    - Examples: almonds, walnuts, chia seeds, flaxseeds, olive oil, avocado

Foods to Avoid or Limit on the DASH Diet

Certain foods should be limited or avoided on the DASH diet due to their high sodium, saturated fat, or added sugar content. Here are the types of foods to minimize in your diet:

- High-sodium foods:
    - Processed and packaged foods, canned soups, salty snacks, and cured meats
    - Examples: potato chips, salted pretzels, canned vegetables with added salt, deli meats
- Saturated fat and trans fat sources:
    - Fatty cuts of meat, full-fat dairy products, and foods containing hydrogenated oils
    - Examples: fatty cuts of beef, pork, full-fat cheese, butter, margarine, pastries
- Added sugars:
    - Sugary beverages, desserts, and processed foods with added sugars
    - Examples: soda, candy, cakes, cookies, ice cream
- Refined grains:
    - Processed grains that have had their nutrient-rich outer layer removed
    - Examples: white bread, white rice, regular pasta, pastries made with white flour

By focusing on nutrient-dense foods and limiting those high in sodium, saturated fat, and added sugars, you can successfully implement the DASH diet and enjoy its numerous health benefits. In the next chapter, we will explore the importance of reducing sodium intake and provide tips on how to do so while following the DASH diet.

4. Sodium and the DASH Diet

The Importance of Reducing Sodium Intake

Reducing sodium intake is a crucial component of the DASH diet, as high sodium consumption is linked to increased blood pressure. Consuming too much sodium can cause your body to retain excess fluid, placing additional strain on your heart and blood vessels. This increased pressure can lead to hypertension and increase the risk of cardiovascular diseases, such as heart attack and stroke.

The American Heart Association recommends that adults consume no more than 2,300 mg of sodium per day, with an ideal limit of 1,500 mg for those with high blood pressure or other risk factors for heart disease. The DASH diet aims to help individuals meet these sodium intake guidelines while still enjoying flavorful, satisfying meals.

Tips for Reducing Sodium Intake on the DASH Diet

Here are some practical tips to help you reduce sodium intake while following the DASH diet:

- Cook at home: Preparing meals at home allows you to control the amount of salt and sodium-containing ingredients used in your dishes.

- Use fresh or frozen produce: Opt for fresh or frozen fruits and vegetables over canned varieties, as canned produce often contains added sodium. If using canned products, choose those labeled "low-sodium" or "no-salt-added," and rinse them before consumption to remove excess sodium.

- Limit processed and packaged foods: These items tend to be high in sodium. Instead, choose whole, unprocessed foods whenever possible.

- Read food labels: Always check the nutrition facts label on packaged foods to understand the sodium content. Look for low-sodium or sodium-free options when shopping.

- Use herbs and spices for flavor: Replace salt with herbs, spices, and other seasonings to add flavor to your meals without increasing sodium intake. Some examples include garlic, onion, black pepper, cumin, paprika, and basil.

- Practice portion control: Even if a food item is relatively low in sodium, consuming large portions can still lead to excessive sodium intake. Be mindful of serving sizes and adjust your intake accordingly.

- Be cautious when dining out: Restaurant meals can be high in sodium. Request that your dishes be prepared with less or no added salt, and choose menu items that are made with whole, fresh ingredients.

- Gradually reduce sodium intake: Slowly reducing your sodium intake can help your taste buds adjust to less salty flavors, making it easier to maintain lower sodium consumption over time.

By following these tips and incorporating the principles of the DASH diet, you can effectively reduce your sodium intake and improve your overall cardiovascular health. In the upcoming chapters, we will provide guidance on meal planning, shopping, and cooking for the DASH diet, as well as share delicious recipes that align with these dietary recommendations.

5. Planning Your DASH Diet Meals

Meal Planning for the DASH Diet

Planning your meals in advance is an effective way to ensure you are consuming a balanced diet that aligns with the DASH guidelines. Follow these steps to create your DASH diet meal plan:

- Set a weekly schedule: Outline your meals and snacks for the week, taking into account your daily routine, work schedule, and social commitments.
- Plan balanced meals: Include a variety of food groups at each meal, aiming to incorporate fruits, vegetables, whole grains, lean protein sources, and low-fat dairy products.
- Plan healthy snacks: Choose nutrient-dense, low-sodium snacks such as fresh fruits, vegetables with hummus, or a handful of unsalted nuts.
- Make a shopping list: Based on your meal plan, create a detailed shopping list that includes all the necessary ingredients.
- Prep ingredients in advance: To save time and make healthy eating more convenient, wash and chop fruits and vegetables, cook whole grains, and prepare lean protein sources ahead of time.
- Be flexible: Life can be unpredictable, so allow for some flexibility in your meal plan. If necessary, swap meals, adjust portion sizes, or substitute ingredients to accommodate changes in your schedule or food availability.

Portion Control and Serving Recommendations

Practicing portion control is essential for managing your sodium intake and ensuring a balanced diet. Here are the daily serving recommendations for each food group on the DASH diet:

- Fruits: 4-5 servings per day
  - 1 serving equals: 1 medium fruit, 1/4 cup dried fruit, or 1/2 cup fresh, frozen, or canned fruit
- Vegetables: 4-5 servings per day
  - 1 serving equals: 1 cup raw leafy greens, 1/2 cup cooked or raw non-leafy vegetables, or 1/2 cup vegetable juice
- Whole grains: 6-8 servings per day
  - 1 serving equals: 1 slice of whole-grain bread, 1/2 cup cooked whole grains (such as rice, pasta, or cereal), or 1 ounce of dry whole grains
- Lean protein sources: 6 or fewer servings per day
  - 1 serving equals: 1 ounce cooked meat, poultry, or fish; 1/4 cup cooked beans or legumes; 1 egg; or 1 tablespoon of peanut butter
- Low-fat or fat-free dairy products: 2-3 servings per day
  - 1 serving equals: 1 cup milk or yogurt, 1.5 ounces of cheese, or 2 ounces of processed cheese
- Nuts, seeds, and healthy fats: 4-5 servings per week
  - 1 serving equals: 1/3 cup nuts, 2 tablespoons seeds, or 2 tablespoons nut butter
- Sweets and added sugars: 5 or fewer servings per week
  - 1 serving equals: 1 tablespoon sugar, 1 tablespoon jelly or jam, or 1/2 cup sorbet

By planning your meals, practicing portion control, and adhering to the DASH diet serving recommendations, you can effectively manage your blood pressure and enjoy a variety of nutritious, delicious foods. In the next chapter, we will share helpful tips for shopping and cooking on the DASH diet.

6. Tips for Success and Overcoming Challenges

Sticking to the DASH diet can be challenging, particularly when dining out, dealing with cravings, and managing social situations. In this chapter, we will share practical advice to help you overcome these challenges and stay committed to the DASH diet.

Tips for Dining Out on the DASH Diet

Eating out can be difficult when following the DASH diet due to the high sodium content in many restaurant dishes. Here are some tips for making healthier choices when dining out:

- Research the menu beforehand: Review the menu online before visiting the restaurant, and identify DASH-friendly options.
- Ask questions: Don't hesitate to ask your server about the ingredients and preparation methods used in a dish. Request modifications if necessary, such as using less salt, butter, or oil.
- Choose wisely: Opt for dishes made with whole, fresh ingredients, such as grilled fish, steamed vegetables, or salads with light dressings.
- Avoid high-sodium options: Stay away from dishes that are fried, breaded, or served with heavy sauces, as they tend to be high in sodium.
- Practice portion control: Restaurant portions can be large, so consider sharing a dish with a companion or packing half of it to take home.

Dealing with Cravings

Cravings can be a challenge when following any diet, including the DASH diet. Here are some strategies for managing cravings:

- Identify your triggers: Recognize the situations, emotions, or times of day that often lead to cravings, and develop a plan for managing them.
- Choose healthy alternatives: When a craving strikes, opt for a DASH-friendly alternative that satisfies your desire for a particular taste or texture, such as fresh fruit for something sweet or crunchy vegetables with hummus for a salty snack.
- Stay hydrated: Drinking water can help curb cravings, as thirst can sometimes be mistaken for hunger.
- Distract yourself: Engage in an activity that takes your mind off the craving, such as going for a walk, calling a friend, or reading a book.

Managing Social Situations

Navigating social situations can be challenging on the DASH diet, but with a little planning and communication, you can enjoy gatherings without compromising your dietary goals:

- Communicate your needs: Inform your friends and family about your dietary restrictions and ask for their support in helping you make healthier choices.
- Offer to bring a dish: Contribute a DASH-friendly dish to gatherings, ensuring you have at least one healthy option to enjoy.
- Focus on moderation: It's okay to indulge in small portions of your favorite treats occasionally. Just remember to balance these indulgences with healthier choices and maintain portion control.
- Enjoy the company: Remember that social gatherings are about connecting with loved ones. Focus on enjoying the conversation and the company, rather than solely on the food.

By implementing these tips and strategies, you can overcome challenges and maintain your commitment to the DASH diet, ultimately reaping the benefits of improved cardiovascular health. In the following chapters, you'll find delicious and nutritious DASH diet recipes to help you on your journey to better health.

7. Physical Activity and Lifestyle Changes

While the DASH diet is a crucial component of managing high blood pressure, physical activity and other lifestyle changes are equally important in promoting overall health. In this chapter, we will discuss the significance of exercise and various lifestyle factors that can help improve your cardiovascular health.

The Importance of Physical Activity

Regular exercise is essential for maintaining a healthy weight, reducing stress, and improving cardiovascular health. It can help lower blood pressure, strengthen your heart, and increase the efficiency of your cardiovascular system. The American Heart Association recommends the following guidelines for physical activity:

- Aim for at least 150 minutes of moderate-intensity aerobic exercise or 75 minutes of vigorous-intensity aerobic exercise per week. Examples of moderate-intensity exercise include brisk walking, cycling, and swimming. Vigorous-intensity activities might include running, high-intensity interval training (HIIT), or playing sports like basketball or soccer.
- Incorporate muscle-strengthening activities, such as resistance training or bodyweight exercises, at least two days per week.

Include flexibility exercises, like stretching or yoga, to promote overall muscle health and prevent injury.

Other Lifestyle Changes for Managing High Blood Pressure

In addition to following the DASH diet and engaging in regular physical activity, consider adopting the following lifestyle changes to further improve your blood pressure and overall health:

- Maintain a healthy weight: Excess weight can contribute to high blood pressure. Losing even a small amount of weight can have a significant impact on lowering your blood pressure.
- Limit alcohol consumption: Drinking alcohol in moderation is key, as excessive consumption can increase blood pressure. Aim to consume no more than one drink per day for women and two drinks per day for men.
- Quit smoking: Smoking is a major risk factor for heart disease and can increase blood pressure. Quitting smoking significantly reduces your risk of cardiovascular problems.
- Manage stress: Chronic stress can contribute to high blood pressure. Incorporate stress-management techniques, such as deep breathing exercises, meditation, or engaging in hobbies, to help reduce your stress levels.
- Get adequate sleep: Aim for 7-9 hours of quality sleep each night, as poor sleep can negatively impact blood pressure and overall health.
- Monitor your blood pressure regularly: Keep track of your blood pressure readings to ensure that your lifestyle changes and the DASH diet are effectively helping you manage your hypertension.

By combining the DASH diet with regular physical activity and adopting these lifestyle changes, you can effectively manage your high blood pressure and improve your overall cardiovascular health. The upcoming chapters will provide you with a range of DASH diet recipes to enjoy as you embark on your journey to better health.

8. 4-week Meal Plan

First Week

DAY	BREAKFAST	LUNCH	DINNER	SNACK
Day-1	Antioxidant Smoothie Bowl (#1)	Gnocchi with Tomato Basil Sauce (#36)	Grilled Chicken with Lemon and Fennel (#75)	Pumpkin Pie Fat Bombs (#106)
Day-2	Fragrant Shakshuka (#2)	Creamy Pumpkin Pasta (#37)	Apple Pie Crackers (#71)	Sweet Almond and Coconut Fat Bombs (#107)
Day-3	Avo Trout Toastie (#3)	Mexican-Style Potato Casserole (#38)	Tantalizing Mushroom Gravy (#73)	Apricot Biscotti (#108)
Day4	Veg Breakfast Taco (#4)	Black Bean Stew with Cornbread (#39)	Everyday Vegetable Stock (#74)	Apple and Berry Cobbler (#109)
Day-5	Colorful Citrus Smoothie (#5)	Mushroom Florentine (#40)	Grilled Chicken with Lemon and Fennel (#75)	Mixed Fruit Compote Cups (#110)
Day-6	Raspberry Polenta Waffles (#6)	Hasselback Eggplant (#41)	Apple Pie Crackers (#71)	Generous Garlic Bread Stick (#111)
Day-7	Stone Fruit Quinoa (#7)	Vegetarian Kebabs (#42)	Tantalizing Mushroom Gravy (#73)	Cauliflower Bread Stick (#112)

Second Week

DAY	BREAKFAST	LUNCH	DINNER	SNACK
Day-1	Fruity Breakfast Muffins (#8)	White Beans Stew (#43)	Humble Mushroom Rice (#77)	Cocktail Wieners (#113)
Day-2	Mushroom Frittata (#9)	Vegetarian Lasagna (#44)	Roasted Root Vegetables with Goat's Cheese Polenta (#78)	Pressure Cooker Braised Pulled Ham (#114)
Day-3	Sweet Potato and Bean Fry Up (#10)	Pan-Fried Salmon with Salad (#45)	Fish Stew (#79)	Mini Teriyaki Turkey Sandwiches (#115)
Day4	Bacon Bits (#11)	Veggie Variety (#46)	Gnocchi Pomodoro (#80)	Peach Crumble Muffins (#116)
Day-5	Steel Cut Oat Blueberry Pancakes (#12)	Vegetable Pasta (#47)	Slow-Cooked Pasta e Fagioli Soup (#81)	Cranberry Hot Wings (#117)
Day-6	Spinach, Mushroom, and Feta Cheese Scramble (#13)	Vegetable Noodles with Bolognese (#48)	Salmon Couscous Salad (#82)	Almond and Tomato Balls (#118)
Day-7	Red Velvet Pancakes with Cream Cheese Topping (#14)	Black Bean Burgers with Lettuce "Buns" (#49)	Roasted Salmon with Smoky Chickpeas and Greens (#83)	Avocado Tuna Bites (#119)

Third Week

DAY	BREAKFAST	LUNCH	DINNER	SNACK
Day-1	Peanut Butter and Banana Breakfast Smoothie (#15)	Curry Vegetable Noodles with Chicken (#50)	Salmon Cakes with Lemon Dill Sauce (#84)	Sweet Potato and Caramelized Onion Flatbread (#120)
Day-2	Greek Yogurt with Honey and Fruits (#16)	Lentil and Vegetable Salad (#51)	Stuffed Bell Peppers (#85)	Zesty Lime and Coconut Energy Balls (#121)
Day-3	Breakfast Quinoa with Berries (#17)	Chickpea Salad (#52)	Spaghetti Carbonara (#86)	Salted Caramel Brownies (#122)
Day4	Breakfast Burrito with Scrambled Eggs and Avocado (#18)	Grilled Chicken with Mango Salsa (#53)	Ratatouille (#87)	Baked Garlic and Herb Zucchini Chips (#123)
Day-5	Veggie Omelette with Fresh Herbs (#19)	Shrimp and Vegetable Stir-Fry (#54)	Lemon Herb Chicken with Roasted Vegetables (#88)	Chocolate Chip Cookie Dough Protein Balls (#124)
Day-6	Chia Seed Pudding with Fresh Fruits (#20)	Quinoa Stuffed Avocado (#55)	Grilled Steak with Chimichurri Sauce (#89)	Crunchy Kale Chips (#125)
Day-7	Savory Spinach and Feta Muffins (#21)	Baked Teriyaki Chicken (#56)	Seared Scallops with Garlic-Lime Butter (#90)	Chocolate Covered Strawberry Greek Yogurt Tarts (#126)

Fourth Week

DAY	BREAKFAST	LUNCH	DINNER	SNACK
1	Apple Cinnamon Overnight Oats (#22)	Greek Salad with Chickpeas and Feta (#57)	Roasted Cauliflower Tacos with Avocado Crema (#91)	Baked Sweet Potato Fries with Chipotle Aioli (#127)
2	Spinach and Cheese Strata (#23)	Thai Green Curry with Vegetables (#58)	Grilled Eggplant with Tomato and Mozzarella (#92)	Roasted Chickpeas with Various Spices (#128)
3	Almond Butter and Banana Toast (#24)	Spicy Black Bean Soup (#59)	Garlic Shrimp and Quinoa (#93)	Cream Cheese and Fruit Stuffed Dates (#129)
4	Broccoli and Cheddar Frittata (#25)	Sushi Bowl with Avocado and Brown Rice (#60)	Mushroom Stroganoff (#94)	Banana and Nut Butter Roll-Ups (#130)
5	Granola and Yogurt Parfait (#26)	Hearty Vegetable Chili (#61)	Chicken Piccata with Capers and Lemon (#95)	Greek Yogurt and Fruit Popsicles (#131)
6	Huevos Rancheros with Avocado Salsa (#27)	Spinach, Strawberry, and Walnut Salad (#62)	Seared Tuna Steaks with Mango Salsa (#96)	Dark Chocolate Almond Clusters (#132)
7	Baked Oatmeal with Berries and Nuts (#28)	Caprese Sandwich with Pesto and Fresh Mozzarella (#63)	Lemon Herb Roasted Chicken and Vegetables (#97)	No-Bake Peanut Butter and Oat Energy Bites (#133)

9. Breakfast

1. Antioxidant Smoothie Bowl

Preparation time: 15 minutes   Cooking time: 0   Servings: 1

Ingredients:

Smoothie:

- 1/2 medium frozen banana, cut into pieces
- 1/2 cup mixed frozen berries (e.g., cherries, blueberries, raspberries)
- 1/2 cup coconut yogurt
- 1 tbsp. pure cocoa powder
- 1 cup fresh chard or spinach
- 1/2 cup unsweetened nut milk (e.g., almond, cashew)

To serve:

- 1/2 tbsp. cocoa nibs
- 1/2 banana, thinly sliced
- 1/4 cup mixed nuts, roughly chopped (e.g., macadamia, almonds, walnuts)

Directions:

1. Blend all the smoothie ingredients on high in a blender until you have a smooth, creamy smoothie. Ensure not to make it too runny by adding the milk little by little.
2. Serve topped with the cocoa nibs, sliced banana, and chopped mixed nuts arranged beautifully, with a sprinkle of cocoa powder to finish.

Nutrition:

Calories: 375   Protein: 11g   Fat: 15g

Carbs: 55g   Sodium: 120mg   Potassium: 500mg

2. Fragrant Shakshuka

Preparation time: 10 minutes   Cooking time: 30 minutes   Servings: 2

Ingredients:

- 1/2 shallot, diced
- 1 clove of garlic, finely chopped
- 1/2 tbsp. olive oil
- 14-ounce jar/tin pre-made, low sodium marinara sauce
- 1/2 cup fresh chard or spinach, chopped
- 4 eggs
- 1/8 cup low-fat feta cheese, crumbled (optional)

Directions:

1. Gently fry the shallot and garlic in the olive oil until the shallots are soft.
2. Add the marinara sauce to the pan. Gently cook the sauce for approximately 20 minutes until nicely reduced and flavorful.
3. Add the chard and stir in.
4. Before the chard has time to overcook, make 4 indents in your sauce, using the back of a large spoon. Crack the eggs into each of these indents. Cover the pan with a lid and gently poach the eggs in the sauce for about 6-8 minutes, until the whites are firm and the yolks are done to your preference.
5. Serve with crumbled feta cheese on top.

Nutrition:

Calories: 310   Protein: 19g   Fat: 19g

Carbs: 12g   Sodium: 430mg   Potassium: 600mg

3. Avo Trout Toastie

Preparation time: 5 minutes   Cooking time: 3 minutes   Servings: 1

Ingredients:

- 1 whole grain bagel, cut in half
- 1/2 large avocado
- 1.5 ounces cold smoked rainbow trout
- Freshly squeezed lemon juice
- Freshly ground black pepper
- Fresh parsley, shredded (optional)
- 1 black cherry tomato or regular cherry tomato, cut into slices

Directions:

1. Gently toast the bagel halves under the grill or in a flat pan on a very low heat.
2. While the bagels toast, cut, peel, and pit the avocado, then place in a bowl with a tablespoon of lemon juice, and smash lightly.
3. To serve: smear the avocado evenly over the bagel halves. Lay the tomato slices down, and top with the smoked trout.
4. Set it off with a generous splash of lemon juice over the fish and some freshly ground black pepper and fresh parsley to taste, if desired.

Nutrition:

Calories: 370	Protein: 21g	Fat: 15g
Carbs: 44g	Sodium: 90mg	Potassium: 450mg

4. Veg Breakfast Tortillas

Preparation time: 5 minutes   Cooking time: 7 minutes   Servings: 2

Ingredients:

- 3 large eggs
- 1/4 cup low-fat milk
- 1 tbsp. olive oil
- 1 small bell pepper (any color), diced
- 1/2 cup baby spinach, fresh
- Black pepper to taste
- 2 small whole wheat tortillas

Directions:

1. Whisk together the eggs, milk, and black pepper in a bowl, and set aside.
2. Warm the olive oil in a pan, then add the diced bell pepper and cook on low heat for about 3 minutes until softened.
3. Add the baby spinach to the pan, turn off the heat, and cover with a lid. Allow spinach to wilt for about 2 minutes.
4. Turn the heat back on and add the egg mixture. Gently stir the eggs until cooked (about 2 minutes).
5. Serve the egg and veggie mixture spooned into the whole wheat tortillas.

Nutrition:

Calories: 340	Protein: 18g	Fat: 19g
Carbs: 23g	Sodium: 190mg	Potassium: 370mg

5. Colorful Citrus Smoothie

Preparation time: 5 minutes   Cooking time: 0 minutes   Servings: 1

Ingredients:

- 1/4 cup cooked, sliced beetroot
- 1/4 cup frozen blueberries
- 1/2 of 1 small orange, peeled and frozen
- 1/2 cup unsweetened almond milk
- 1 tbsp. chia seeds
- 1/2 cup low-fat Greek yogurt
- 3-4 ice cubes

Directions:

1. Blend the almond milk and chia seeds together on low for 20-30 seconds.
2. Add the remaining ingredients and blend on high until thick, smooth, and creamy.

Nutrition:

Calories: 240	Protein: 17g	Fat: 7g
Carbs: 30g	Sodium: 120mg	Potassium: 600mg

6. Raspberry Polenta Waffles

Preparation time: 15 minutes   Cooking time: 20 minutes   Servings: 2

Ingredients:

- 1/2 tbsp. unsalted butter, melted
- 1/2 cup low-fat milk
- 1/2 cup plain cake flour
- 1/2 cup finely ground polenta
- 3/4 tsp. baking powder
- 1 large egg white
- 1 cup low-fat, plain yogurt
- 3 ounces raspberries, for serving

Directions:

1. Mix the milk and melted butter together in a bowl.
2. Sift the flour, polenta, and baking powder into a separate bowl, whisk gently, then stir in the milk mixture until just combined. Set aside.

3. Preheat your waffle iron.
4. In an electric mixer, whip the egg white until stiff peaks form. Gently fold the egg white into the flour mixture.
5. Lightly grease the waffle iron, and then add about 1/2 cup of the waffle batter into the iron. Close and let cook until they are golden brown and cooked through.
6. To serve, place 1 waffle on each plate. Spoon 1/2 cup yogurt over them and cascade a handful of raspberries over the top.
7. Enjoy warm!

Nutrition:

Calories: 410	Fiber: 4g	Potassium: 300mg
Carbs: 65g	Sodium: 400mg	
Protein: 18g	Fat: 9g	

7. Stone Fruit Quinoa

Preparation time: 5 minutes   Cooking time: 20 minutes   Servings: 2

Ingredients:

- 1/2 cup finely chopped fresh apricots
- 1/4 tsp. ground cinnamon
- 1 cup low-fat milk
- 1/2 cup quinoa, rinsed and drained
- 1 tbsp. chopped pecan nuts
- 1 tbsp. honey

Directions:

1. Place the apricots, cinnamon, milk, and quinoa in a medium pot, and bring to a boil.
2. Set the heat to low and cook for about 20 minutes. The quinoa will absorb most of the liquid by this stage.
3. Set off the heat and let stand with the lid on for about 5 minutes.
4. Using a fork, incorporate air into the quinoa by whisking gently.
5. Serve hot, with pecans sprinkled over it and a drizzle of honey to sweeten.

Nutrition:

Calories: 370	Protein: 14g	Fat: 10g
Carbs: 58g	Sodium: 80mg	Potassium: 600mg

8. Fruity Breakfast Muffins

Preparation time: 15 minutes   Cooking time: 22 minutes   Servings: 2

Ingredients:

- 1/2 cup cake flour
- 1/4 cup rolled oats
- 1/2 tsp. baking powder
- 1 ripe banana
- 1/6 cup castor sugar
- 1/8 cup sunflower oil
- 1/2 cup fresh cranberries

Directions:

1. Preheat the oven to 350F.
2. Combine the cake flour, baking powder, and rolled oats in a bowl.
3. In another bowl, mash up the banana, then add the caster sugar. Mix well, then add the sunflower oil and whisk to combine.
4. Mix the dry and wet ingredients in a bowl, then add the cranberries.
5. Grease a 2-cup muffin tray or use silicone muffin cups, then divide the mixture evenly amongst the muffin cups.
6. Bake for about 20-22 minutes, or until, when a skewer is inserted into the middle, it comes out clean.

Nutrition:

Calories: 305	Protein: 5g	Fat: 11g
Carbs: 47g	Sodium: 95mg	Potassium: 200mg

9. Mushroom Frittata

Preparation time: 10 minutes   Cooking time: 10 minutes   Servings: 2

Ingredients:

- 1 tsp. unsalted butter, melted
- 1 large brown mushroom, sliced
- 1/2 cup chopped oyster mushroom
- 2 tbsp. minced onion

- 3 large eggs
- 1/2 cup low-fat Greek yogurt (as a substitute for sour cream)
- Black pepper to taste

Directions:

1. Melt the butter in a medium non-stick pan over medium heat.
2. Add the onion and mushrooms to the pan and cook gently for 3-4 minutes.
3. In a separate bowl, whisk together the eggs and low-fat Greek yogurt until well combined. Add black pepper to taste.
4. Turn on the broiler function on your oven and allow it to heat.
5. Pour the egg mixture into the pan and cook gently on low for 2 minutes.
6. Place the pan under the broiler for about 1-2 minutes until the top of your frittata is a beautiful golden color.
7. To serve, loosen the edges of the frittata using a spatula. Place a large plate over the top of the pan and then invert it, allowing the frittata to turn over onto the plate.
8. Cut and serve warm.

Nutrition:

Calories: 232	Protein: 18g	Fat: 15g
Carbs: 7g	Sodium: 129mg	Potassium: 240mg

10. Sweet Potato and Bean Fry Up

Preparation time: 10 minutes   Cooking time: 10 minutes   Servings: 2

Ingredients:

- 1 cup sweet potato, washed and diced
- 1 tbsp. olive oil
- 1/2 can of red kidney beans (approx. 7.5 ounces), rinsed and drained
- 1 cup grated zucchini (as a substitute for rice zucchini)
- 2 cups baby spinach, finely chopped
- 4 cherry tomatoes, halved
- Black pepper to taste

Directions:

1. In a medium-sized pan with high sides, heat the olive oil until a piece of sweet potato placed in the pan sizzles. Add the sweet potato and fry on medium heat for about 5 minutes until browned and cooked through.
2. Add in the grated zucchini, red kidney beans, and cherry tomatoes. Cook for about 4 minutes until all the ingredients have heated through. Then add the baby spinach, and wilt for 1 minute. Add black pepper to taste.
3. Serve hot.

Nutrition:

Calories: 285	Protein: 11g	Fat: 10g
Carbs: 41g	Sodium: 45mg	Potassium: 179mg

11. Bacon Bits

Preparation time: 15 minutes   Cooking time: 60 minutes   Servings: 2

Ingredients:

- 1/2 cup Millet
- 2.5 cups water
- 1/2 cup sweet potato, diced
- 1/2 tsp. cinnamon, ground
- 1 tbsp. brown sugar
- 1/2 medium apple, diced
- 2 tbsp. honey

Directions:

1. In a deep pot, combine sugar, sweet potato, cinnamon, water, and millet, then stir to mix, and bring to a boil on high heat. After that, reduce heat and simmer on low.
2. Cook for about an hour until the water is fully absorbed and the millet is cooked. Stir in the diced apple and serve drizzled with honey.

Nutrition:

Calories: 136	Protein: 3.1g	Sodium: 60mg
Carbs: 30g	Fat: 1.0g	Potassium: 120mg

12. Steel Cut Oat Blueberry Pancakes

Preparation time: 15 minutes   Cooking time: 15 minutes   Servings: 2

Ingredients:

- 3/4 cup water
- 1/4 cup steel-cut oats
- 1/2 cup whole-wheat flour
- 1/4 tsp. baking powder
- 1/4 tsp. baking soda
- 1 egg
- 1/2 cup blueberries, frozen

Directions:

1. Combine the oats, water in a medium saucepan, stir, and bring to a boil over high heat. Adjust the heat to low, and let it simmer for about 10 minutes or until the oats become tender. Set aside.
2. In a medium bowl, mix the whole-wheat flour, baking powder, baking soda, and egg. Then, fold in the cooked oats and blueberries.
3. Preheat a skillet and lightly grease it. Cook 1/4 cup of the batter at a time for about 3 minutes per side.

Nutrition:

Calories: 191   Protein: 9g   Sodium: 61.5mg

Carbs: 33g   Fat: 3g   Potassium: 130mg

13. Spinach, Mushroom, and Feta Cheese Scramble

Preparation time: 15 minutes   Cooking time: 4 minutes   Servings: 1

Ingredients:

- Olive oil cooking spray
- 1/4 cup mushroom, sliced
- 1/2 cup spinach, chopped
- 2 eggs
- 1 tbsp. Feta cheese
- Pepper

Directions:

1. Lightly grease a medium skillet with olive oil cooking spray and set it over medium heat. Add spinach and mushrooms, and cook until the spinach wilts.
2. In a medium bowl, whisk together the eggs, feta cheese, and pepper. Pour the mixture into the skillet and cook, stirring occasionally, until set for about 4 minutes.
3. Serve.

Nutrition:

Calories: 181   Protein: 15.1g   Sodium: 52.5mg

Carbs: 6.5g   Fat: 11g   Potassium: 120mg

14. Red Velvet Pancakes with Cream Cheese Topping

Preparation time: 15 minutes   Cooking time: 10 minutes   Servings: 2

Ingredients:

Cream Cheese Topping:

- 1 oz. cream cheese
- 1.5 tbsp. yogurt
- 1.5 tbsp. honey

Pancakes:

- 1/2 cup whole wheat flour
- 3/4 tsp. baking powder
- 1/2 cup milk
- 1 large egg
- 1/2 tsp. red paste food coloring

Directions:

1. In a medium bowl, combine cream cheese, yogurt, and honey. Set aside.
2. In a large bowl, mix whole wheat flour, baking powder, milk, egg, and red paste food coloring until combined.
3. Heat a greased skillet over medium heat. Pour 1/4 cup of pancake batter onto the hot skillet and cook until bubbles begin to form on the top. Flip and cook until set. Repeat until all the batter is used.
4. Serve pancakes with cream cheese topping.

Nutrition:

Calories: 295   Carbs: 39.9g   Sodium: 226mg

Protein: 10.5g   Fat: 9.5g   Potassium: 135mg

15. Peanut Butter and Banana Breakfast Smoothie

Preparation time: 15 minutes   Cooking time: 0 minutes   Servings: 1

Ingredients:

- 1 cup non-fat milk
- 1 tbsp. peanut butter
- 1 banana
- 1/2 tsp. vanilla

Directions:

1. Combine non-fat milk, peanut butter, banana, and vanilla in a blender. Blend until smooth.

Nutrition:

Calories: 295   Carbs: 4.2 g   Sodium: 100 mg
Protein: 133 g   Fat: 8.4 g   Potassium: 143mg

16. No-Bake Breakfast Granola Bars

Preparation time: 15 minutes   Cooking time: 0 minutes   Servings: 2

Ingredients:

- 2/3 cup oatmeal, old fashioned
- 1/4 cup raisins
- 1/4 cup brown sugar
- 1 1/4 cup corn rice cereal
- 1/4 cup syrup
- 1/4 cup peanut butter
- 1/2 tsp. vanilla

Directions:

1. In a mixing bowl, combine rice cereal, oatmeal, and raisins using a wooden spoon.
2. In a saucepan, combine corn syrup and brown sugar. Over medium-high heat, continuously stir the mixture and bring to a boil.
3. Once boiling, remove from heat. Add vanilla and peanut butter to the sugar mixture. Stir until smooth.
4. Pour the peanut butter mixture over the cereal and raisins in the mixing bowl, and combine well.
5. Press the mixture into a small baking dish. Allow it to cool completely, and then cut into 2 bars.

Nutrition:

Calories: 152   Carbs: 2.6 g   Sodium: 90 mg
Protein: 4 g   Fat: 4.3 g   Potassium: 189mg

17. Mushroom Shallot Frittata

Preparation time: 15 minutes   Cooking time: 25 minutes   Servings: 2

Ingredients:

- 1/2 tsp unsalted butter
- 2 shallots, chopped
- 1/4 lb. mushrooms, chopped
- 1 tsp. parsley, chopped
- 1/2 tsp. thyme, dried
- Black pepper
- 2 large eggs
- 1/8 cup grated parmesan cheese

Directions:

1. Preheat oven to 350F. In a suitable size oven-proof skillet, heat butter over medium flame. Add shallots and sauté for about 5 minutes, or until golden brown. Add mushrooms, parsley, thyme, and black pepper to taste.
2. Whisk eggs and parmesan cheese in a bowl. Pour the mixture into the skillet, ensuring that the mushrooms are completely covered. Transfer the skillet to the oven as soon as the edges begin to set.
3. Bake for 15-20 minutes.

Nutrition:

Calories: 174   Carbs: 8 g   Sodium: 200 mg
Protein: 12 g   Fat: 11 g   Potassium: 350 mg

18. Jack-o-Lantern Pancakes

Preparation time: 15 minutes   Cooking time: 5 minutes   Servings: 2

Ingredients:

- 1/4 egg (use 1 small egg or whisk a large egg and use half)
- 1/4 cup pumpkin puree, canned

- 7/8 cup low-fat milk
- 1 tbsp. vegetable oil
- 1 cup whole-wheat flour
- 1 tbsp. brown sugar
- 1/2 tbsp. baking powder

Directions:
1. In a mixing bowl, combine milk, pumpkin puree, egg, and oil. Add dry ingredients (whole-wheat flour, brown sugar, and baking powder) to the egg mixture. Stir gently. Lightly coat a skillet with cooking spray and heat on medium.
2. When the skillet is hot, pour batter onto the skillet. When bubbles start bursting, flip pancakes over and cook until golden-brown.

Nutrition:
Calories: 480
Protein: 17 g
Carbs: 70 g
Fat: 17 g
Sodium: 250 mg
Potassium: 380 mg

19. Fruit Pizza

Preparation time: 15 minutes Cooking time: 0 minutes Servings: 2

Ingredients:
- 1 English muffin
- 2 tbsp. fat-free cream cheese
- 2 tbsp. strawberries, sliced
- 2 tbsp. blueberries
- 2 tbsp. pineapple, crushed

Directions:
1. Divide English muffin in half and toast halves until slightly browned.
2. Coat both halves with cream cheese. Set fruits atop cream cheese on muffin halves.
3. Serve soon after preparation.

Nutrition:
Calories: 119
Protein: 6 g
Carbs: 2.3 g
Fat: 1 g
Sodium: 28 mg
Potassium: 180mg

20. Flax Banana Yogurt Muffins

Preparation time: 15 minutes Cooking time: 20 minutes Servings: 2

Ingredients:
- 1/3 cup whole wheat flour
- 1/3 cup old-fashioned oats, rolled
- 1/4 tsp. baking soda
- 1 tbsp. flaxseed, ground
- 1 large ripe banana
- 1/4 cup Greek yogurt
- 1/8 cup applesauce, unsweetened

Directions:
1. Preheat oven to 355°F. Prepare a muffin tin with cooking spray or cupcake liners. In a mixing bowl, combine whole wheat flour, rolled oats, baking soda, and ground flaxseed.
2. In a separate bowl, mash the ripe banana and mix it with Greek yogurt and unsweetened applesauce. Combine the wet and dry mixtures and mix gently. Do not overmix. Divide the batter between 4 muffin cups in the prepared tin. Bake for 20 minutes, or until a toothpick inserted comes out clean.

Nutrition:
Calories: 220
Protein: 8 g
Carbs: 40 g
Fat: 4 g
Sodium: 150 mg
Potassium: 350 mg

21. Apple Oats

Preparation time: 5 minutes Cooking time: 5 minutes Servings: 2

Ingredients:
- 1/2 cup oats
- 1 cup water
- 1 apple, chopped
- 1/2 tsp. cinnamon
- 1/2 tsp. vanilla extract

Directions:
1. In a saucepan, combine oats and water. Bring to a boil over medium heat.
2. Once boiling, reduce the heat to low and cook the oats for 5 minutes, stirring occasionally.

3. Add the chopped apples, cinnamon, and vanilla extract. Stir well to combine. Cook for another 1-2 minutes to soften the apples slightly.
4. Serve warm.

Nutrition:

Calories: 150	Carbs: 30 g	Sodium: 5 mg
Protein: 4 g	Fat: 2 g	Potassium: 300 mg

22. Buckwheat Crepes

Preparation time: 5 minutes   Cooking time: 5 minutes   Servings: 2

Ingredients:

- 1/2 cup buckwheat flour
- 1/4 cup whole grain flour
- 1 egg, beaten
- 1/2 cup skim milk
- 1/4 tsp. cinnamon, ground

Directions:

1. In a mixing bowl, combine buckwheat flour, whole grain flour, beaten egg, skim milk, and cinnamon. Whisk until you get a smooth batter.
2. Heat a non-stick skillet over medium-high heat.
3. Pour a small amount of batter into the skillet and swirl it around to form a thin crepe.
4. Cook for 1 minute, then flip and cook the other side for another 1 minute or until golden brown.
5. Repeat the same steps with the remaining batter, making a total of 2-3 crepes depending on the size.

Nutrition:

Calories: 180	Carbs: 31 g	Sodium: 45 mg
Protein: 8 g	Fat: 3 g	Potassium: 260 mg

23. Whole Grain Pancakes

Preparation time: 10 minutes   Cooking time: 5 minutes   Servings: 2

Ingredients:

- 1/4 tsp. baking powder
- 1/8 cup skim milk
- 1/2 cup whole-grain wheat flour
- 1 tsp. liquid honey
- 1/2 tsp. olive oil

Directions:

1. Combine baking powder and flour in a bowl.
2. Add skim milk and olive oil. Whisk the mixture well.
3. Heat a non-stick skillet over medium heat and pour a small amount of batter into the skillet, forming a pancake. Cook for about 2 minutes on each side, until the pancake is golden brown.
4. Repeat the process with the remaining batter, making a total of 2-3 pancakes, depending on the size.
5. Top the cooked pancakes with liquid honey before serving.

Nutrition:

Calories: 135	Carbs: 25 g	Sodium: 5 mg
Protein: 5 g	Fat: 2 g	Potassium: 100 mg

24. Granola Parfait

Preparation time: 10 minutes   Cooking time: 0 minutes   Servings: 2

Ingredients:

- 1/2 cup low-fat yogurt
- 4 tbsp. granola

Directions:

1. Put 1/2 tbsp. of granola in every glass.
2. Then add 2 tbsp. of low-fat yogurt.
3. Redo the steps till you use all ingredients.
4. Set the parfait in the fridge for up to 2 hours.

Nutrition:

| Calories: 79 | Carbs: 20.6 g | Sodium: 51 mg |
| Protein: 8 g | Fat: 8.1 g | Potassium: 134mg |

25. Curry Tofu Scramble

Preparation time: 10 minutes   Cooking time: 5 minutes   Servings: 2

Ingredients:

- 8 oz. tofu, crumbled
- 1/2 tsp. curry powder
- 1/8 cup skim milk
- 1/2 tsp. olive oil
- 1/8 tsp. chili flakes

Directions:

1. Heat olive oil in a skillet over medium heat.
2. Add crumbled tofu and chili flakes, and cook for 2-3 minutes, stirring occasionally.
3. In a small bowl, combine curry powder and skim milk.
4. Pour the curry milk mixture over the crumbled tofu, stirring well to evenly coat the tofu.
5. Cook the scrambled tofu on medium-high heat for an additional 2-3 minutes, until heated through.

Nutrition:

| Calories: 102 | Carbs: 3 g | Sodium: 25 mg |
| Protein: 10 g | Fat: 6 g | Potassium: 80 mg |

26. Easy Veggie Muffins

Preparation time: 10 minutes   Cooking time: 40 minutes   Servings: 2

Ingredients:

- 1/2 cup cheddar cheese, shredded
- 1/2 cup green onion, chopped
- 1/2 cup tomatoes, chopped
- 1/2 cup broccoli, chopped
- 1 cup non-fat milk
- 1/2 cup biscuit mix
- 2 eggs
- Cooking spray

Directions:

1. Preheat the oven to 375F. Coat a muffin tray with cooking spray.
2. Divide broccoli, tomatoes, cheese, and green onions equally among four muffin cups.
3. In a bowl, combine milk, biscuit mix, and eggs. Whisk well and pour the mixture into the muffin cups, filling each one evenly.
4. Bake for 40 minutes, or until a toothpick inserted in the center comes out clean. Remove the muffins from the oven and let them cool slightly before serving.

Nutrition:

| Calories: 240 | Protein: 15 g | Sodium: 50 mg |
| Carbs: 18 g | Fat: 10 g | Potassium: 156 mg |

27. Carrot Muffins

Preparation time: 10 minutes   Cooking time: 30 minutes   Servings: 5

Ingredients:

- 3/4 cup whole wheat flour
- 1/4 cup stevia
- 1/2 tsp. baking powder
- 1/4 tsp. cinnamon powder
- 1/4 cup natural apple juice
- 1 carrot, grated
- Cooking spray

Directions:

1. Preheat the oven to 375F. In a large bowl, combine the whole wheat flour, stevia, baking powder, and cinnamon powder.
2. Add the apple juice and grated carrot to the flour mixture and stir until well combined.
3. Coat a muffin tray with cooking spray, then divide the muffin mixture evenly among two muffin cups.
4. Bake for 30 minutes, or until a toothpick inserted in the center comes out clean. Allow the muffins to cool slightly before serving.

Nutrition:

| Calories: 340 | Fat: 2 g | Sodium: 104 mg |
| Carbs: 72 g | Protein: 10 g | Potassium: 240 mg |

28. Pineapple Oatmeal

Preparation time: 10 minutes   Cooking time: 25 minutes   Servings: 2

Ingredients:
- 1 cup old-fashioned oats
- 1/2 cup pineapple, cubed
- 1/2 cup non-fat milk
- 1 egg
- 1 tbsp. stevia
- 1 tsp. vanilla extract
- Cooking spray

Directions:
1. Preheat the oven to 400F. In a bowl, combine the oats with the pineapple. Stir and divide the mixture into 2 ramekins coated with cooking spray.
2. In another bowl, whisk the non-fat milk with the egg, stevia, and vanilla extract. Pour this mixture over the oats in the ramekins.
3. Bake for 25 minutes, or until the oatmeal is set and lightly golden. Serve for breakfast.

Nutrition:

| Calories: 300 | Fat: 5 g | Sodium: 80 mg |
| Carbs: 48 g | Protein: 13 g | Potassium: 270 mg |

29. Spinach Muffins

Preparation time: 10 minutes   Cooking time: 30 minutes   Servings: 6

Ingredients:
- 2 eggs
- 1/6 cup non-fat milk
- 1/3 cup low-fat cheese, crumbled
- 1.3 oz. spinach, chopped
- 1/6 cup red pepper, roasted and chopped
- 0.67 oz. prosciutto, chopped
- Cooking spray

Directions:
1. Preheat the oven to 350F. In a bowl, whisk the eggs with the non-fat milk. Stir in the low-fat cheese, chopped spinach, roasted red pepper, and prosciutto.
2. Coat a muffin tray with cooking spray and divide the mixture evenly into 2 muffin cups.
3. Bake for 30 minutes, or until the muffins are set and lightly golden. Remove from the oven, let them cool slightly, and serve for breakfast.

Nutrition:

| Calories: 224 | Fat: 6 g | Sodium: 88 mg |
| Carbs: 3.8 g | Protein: 4 g | Potassium: 280 mg |

30. Chia Seeds Breakfast Mix

Preparation time: 8 hours   Cooking time: 0 minutes   Servings: 2

Ingredients:
- 1 cup old-fashioned oats
- 2 tbsp. chia seeds
- 2 tbsp. coconut sugar
- 1/2 cup blueberries
- 1.5 cups unsweetened almond milk (replacing coconut milk to reduce saturated fat)
- 1/2 tsp. lemon zest, grated

Directions:
1. In a bowl, combine the oats, chia seeds, coconut sugar, almond milk, lemon zest, and blueberries. Stir well to mix the ingredients.
2. Divide the mixture into two cups or containers and place them in the refrigerator for 8 hours or overnight.
3. Serve chilled.

Nutrition:

| Calories: 380 | Fat: 11 g | Sodium: 45 mg |
| Carbs: 61 g | Protein: 12 g | Potassium: 295 mg |

31. Breakfast Fruits Bowls

Preparation time: 10 minutes | Cooking time: 0 minutes | Servings: 2

Ingredients:

- 1 cup mango, chopped
- 1 banana, sliced
- 1 cup pineapple, chopped
- 1 cup unsweetened almond milk

Directions:

1. In a bowl, combine the chopped mango, sliced banana, chopped pineapple, and unsweetened almond milk. Stir well to mix the ingredients.
2. Divide the mixture into two smaller bowls and serve immediately.

Nutrition:

| Calories: 190 | Fat: 2 g | Sodium: 80 mg |
| Carbs: 43 g | Protein: 2 g | Potassium: 580 mg |

32. Pumpkin Cookies

Preparation time: 10 minutes | Cooking time: 25 minutes | Servings: 2

Ingredients:

- 2/3 cup whole wheat flour
- 1/3 cup old-fashioned oats
- 1/2 tsp. baking soda
- 1/2 tsp. pumpkin pie spice
- 5 oz. pumpkin puree
- 1/3 cup coconut oil, melted
- 1/3 cup coconut sugar

Directions:

1. Preheat the oven to 350°F (175°C). In a bowl, mix the whole wheat flour, oats, baking soda, pumpkin pie spice, pumpkin puree, melted coconut oil, and coconut sugar. Stir well to combine.
2. Shape the mixture into 4 medium-sized cookies and arrange them on a baking sheet lined with parchment paper.
3. Bake for 25 minutes, or until the cookies are firm and lightly golden. Allow the cookies to cool before serving.

Nutrition:

| Calories: 575 | Fat: 32 g | Sodium: 230 mg |
| Carbs: 72 g | Protein: 9 g | Potassium: 400 mg |

33. Veggie Scramble

Preparation time: 10 minutes | Cooking time: 2 minutes | Servings: 1

Ingredients:

- 1 egg
- 1 tbsp. water
- 1/4 cup broccoli, chopped
- 1/4 cup mushrooms, chopped
- A pinch black pepper
- 1 tbsp. low-fat mozzarella, shredded
- Cooking spray

Directions:

1. Grease a microwave-safe ramekin with cooking spray. Add the egg, water, pepper, mushrooms, and broccoli. Whisk well to combine.
2. Microwave the ramekin for 2 minutes or until the egg is cooked through. The cooking time may vary depending on the microwave, so check the egg after 1 minute and then in 30-second increments.
3. Sprinkle the shredded low-fat mozzarella on top of the cooked egg mixture. Serve immediately.

Nutrition:

| Calories: 113 | Fat: 6 g | Sodium: 150 mg |
| Carbs: 6 g | Protein: 10 g | Potassium: 350 mg |

34. Mushrooms and Turkey Breakfast

Preparation time: 10 minutes   Cooking time: 50 minutes   Servings: 2

Ingredients:

- 2 oz. whole-wheat bread, cubed
- 3 oz. turkey sausage, chopped
- 1/2 cup fat-free milk
- 1.5 oz. low-fat cheddar, shredded
- 1 egg
- 1/4 cup mushrooms, chopped
- 1/4 cup green onions, chopped

Directions:

1. Preheat the oven to 400°F (200°C). Put the bread cubes on a lined baking sheet and bake for 8 minutes. Meanwhile, in a pan over medium-high heat, cook the turkey sausage, stirring, until browned (about 7 minutes).
2. In a bowl, whisk together the milk, shredded cheddar, and egg.
3. Add the mushrooms, cooked turkey sausage, bread cubes, and green onions to the milk mixture, and stir well.
4. Pour the mixture into a small greased baking dish and bake at 350°F (175°C) for about 25-30 minutes, or until set and the top is golden.
5. Slice, divide between plates, and serve for breakfast.

Nutrition:

Calories: 268   Fat: 12 g   Sodium: 370 mg
Carbs: 21 g   Protein: 20 g   Potassium: 334 mg

35. Mushrooms and Cheese Omelet

Preparation time: 10 minutes   Cooking time: 10 minutes   Servings: 2

Ingredients:

- 1 tbsp. olive oil
- 1.5 oz. mushrooms, sliced
- 1/2 cup baby spinach, chopped
- 2 eggs, whisked
- 1 tbsp. low-fat cheese, grated
- 1/2 small avocado, peeled, pitted, and cubed
- A pinch of black pepper

Directions:

1. Heat the olive oil in a pan over medium-high heat. Add the mushrooms, stir, and cook for 5 minutes. Transfer the cooked mushrooms to a bowl.
2. In the same pan over medium-high heat, add the whisked eggs and black pepper, spreading them evenly in the pan. Cook for about 3-4 minutes or until the eggs are set.
3. Place the spinach, cooked mushrooms, avocado, and grated cheese on one half of the omelet. Fold the other half of the omelet over the filling.
4. Slide the omelet onto a plate and serve.

Nutrition:

Calories: 226   Fat: 17 g   Sodium: 146 mg
Carbs: 7 g   Protein: 10 g   Potassium: 259 mg

10. Lunch

36. Gnocchi with Tomato Basil Sauce

Preparation time: 15 minutes   Cooking time: 25 minutes   Servings: 2

Ingredients:

- 1 tbsp. olive oil
- 1/4 yellow onion, peeled and diced
- 1 clove garlic, peeled and minced
- 1 cup no-salt-added canned tomatoes, crushed
- 1/8 cup fresh basil leaves
- 1 tsp. Italian seasoning
- 4 oz. gnocchi

Directions:

1. Heat the olive oil in a stockpot over medium heat. Add the onion and sauté for 5 to 6 minutes until soft. Stir in the garlic and cook until fragrant, 30 to 60 seconds. Then stir in the tomatoes, basil, and Italian seasoning.
2. Bring to a simmer for 15 minutes. For a smooth, puréed sauce, use an immersion blender or transfer sauce to a blender and purée until smooth. Taste and adjust the seasoning, if necessary.
3. While the sauce simmers, cook the gnocchi according to the package instructions, remove with a slotted spoon, and transfer to 2 bowls. Pour the sauce over the gnocchi.

Nutrition:

Calories: 277   Fat: 9 g   Protein: 6 g
Carbs: 40 g   Sodium: 67 mg   Potassium: 313 mg

37. Creamy Pumpkin Pasta

Preparation time: 15 minutes   Cooking time: 30 minutes   Servings: 2

Ingredients:

- 5 oz. whole-grain linguine
- 1 tsp. olive oil
- 1 garlic clove, peeled and minced
- 1/2 cup pumpkin purée
- 1/3 cup unsalted vegetable stock
- 1/4 cup low-fat evaporated milk
- 1 tbsp. fresh sage, chopped

Directions:

1. Cook the whole-grain linguine in a large pot of boiling water. Reserve 1/4 cup of pasta water and drain the rest. Set the pasta aside.
2. Heat the olive oil over medium heat in a large skillet. Add the garlic and sage, and sauté for 1 to 2 minutes, until soft and fragrant. Whisk in the pumpkin purée, stock, milk, and reserved pasta water, and simmer for 4 to 5 minutes, until thickened.
3. Stir in the cooked whole-grain linguine. Evenly divide the pasta between 2 bowls.

Nutrition:

Calories: 397   Fat: 7 g   Protein: 17 g
Carbs: 72 g   Sodium: 73 mg   Potassium: 372 mg

38. Mexican-Style Potato Casserole

Preparation time: 15 minutes   Cooking time: 60 minutes   Servings: 8

Ingredients:

- Cooking spray
- 1 tsp. canola oil
- 1/4 yellow onion, peeled and diced
- 2 garlic cloves, peeled and minced
- 3/4 cup milk
- 3/4 cup Mexican-style cheese, shredded and divided
- 3/4 lb. baby Yukon Gold or red potatoes, thinly sliced

Directions:

1. Preheat the oven to 400°F. Grease a small baking dish with cooking spray. In a large saucepan, heat canola oil on medium heat. Add the onion and sauté for 4 to 5 minutes until soft. Mix in the garlic, then cook until fragrant, 30 to 60 seconds.

2. Pour in the milk and bring to a gentle simmer. Cook for about 5 minutes until slightly thickened. Remove from the heat and whisk in half of the shredded cheese.
3. Arrange half of the sliced potatoes in the baking dish and top with a quarter of the remaining shredded cheese. Layer the remaining potatoes on top, and then sprinkle with another quarter of the shredded cheese.
4. Pour the cheese sauce over the top and sprinkle with the remaining shredded cheese. Cover with aluminum foil and bake for 45 to 50 minutes, until the potatoes are tender.
5. Remove the foil and bake for an additional 5 to 10 minutes, until the topping is slightly browned. Let cool for 20 minutes before serving.

Nutrition:

Calories: 410

Fat: 25 g

Protein: 17 g

Carbs: 31 g

Sodium: 390 mg

Potassium: 892 mg

39. Black Bean Stew with Cornbread

Preparation time: 15 minutes   Cooking time: 55 minutes   Servings: 2

Ingredients:

For the black bean stew:

- 1 tsp. canola oil
- 1/2 yellow onion, peeled and diced
- 1 garlic clove, peeled and minced
- 1 can no-salt-added black beans, drained
- 1/2 (10-oz.) can tomatoes, fire-roasted, diced
- 1/2 tbsp. chili powder
- 1/2 tbsp. ground cumin

For the cornbread topping:

- 1/2 cup cornmeal
- 1/4 cup all-purpose flour
- 1/4 tsp. baking powder
- 1/2 cup low-fat buttermilk
- 1 large egg

Directions:

1. Heat the canola oil over medium heat in a small pot. Add the onion and sauté for 4 to 6 minutes, until the onion is soft. Stir in the garlic, chili powder, and cumin.
2. Add the black beans and diced tomatoes. Bring to a simmer and cook for 15 minutes.
3. Preheat the oven to 375°F. While the stew simmers, prepare the cornbread topping. Mix the cornmeal, all-purpose flour, and baking powder in a bowl. In a measuring cup, whisk the buttermilk and egg until combined. Add the wet mixture to the dry ingredients and mix until just combined.
4. In an oven-safe bowl or dish, spoon out the black bean stew. Dollop the cornbread batter on top and then spread it out evenly with a spatula. Bake for 30 minutes, until the cornbread is just set.

Nutrition:

Calories: 500

Fat: 10 g

Protein: 23 g

Carbs: 81 g

Sodium: 160 mg

Potassium: 1110 mg

40. Mushroom Florentine

Preparation time: 15 minutes   Cooking time: 20 minutes   Servings: 2

Ingredients:

- 2.5 oz. whole-grain pasta
- 1/8 cup low-sodium vegetable broth
- 1/2 cup mushrooms, sliced
- 1/8 cup soy milk
- 1/4 tsp. Italian seasonings

Directions:

1. Cook the pasta according to the manufacturer's directions. Set aside.
2. In a saucepan, heat the vegetable broth over medium heat. Add mushrooms and Italian seasonings. Cook the mushrooms for 10 minutes, stirring occasionally.
3. Add soy milk to the saucepan and mix well. Add the cooked pasta, stirring to combine with the mushroom mixture. Cook for an additional 5 minutes on low heat.

Nutrition:

Calories: 188

Protein: 7 g

Sodium: 17 mg

Carbs: 36 g

Fat: 1.4 g

Potassium: 97 mg

41. Hassel back Eggplant

Preparation time: 15 minutes   Cooking time: 25 minutes   Servings: 2

Ingredients:

- 2 eggplants, trimmed
- 2 tomatoes, sliced
- 1 tbsp. low-fat yogurt
- 1 tsp. curry powder
- 1 tsp. olive oil

Directions:

1. Make cuts in the eggplants in the shape of Hasselback. Rub the eggplants with curry powder and stuff with sliced tomatoes.
2. Drizzle the eggplants with olive oil and yogurt. Wrap each Hasselback eggplant separately in foil.
3. Bake the eggplants at 375°F (190°C) for 25 minutes.

Nutrition:

Calories: 188   Carbs: 34 g   Sodium: 23 mg

Protein: 7 g   Fat: 7 g   Potassium: 137 mg

42. Vegetarian Kebabs

Preparation time: 15 minutes   Cooking time: 6 minutes   Servings: 2

Ingredients:

- 1 tbsp. balsamic vinegar
- 1/2 tbsp. olive oil
- 1/2 tsp. dried parsley
- 1 sweet pepper
- 1 red onion, peeled
- 1 zucchini, trimmed

Directions:

1. Cut the sweet pepper and onion into medium-sized squares. Slice the zucchini. Thread all vegetables onto skewers. In a shallow bowl, mix olive oil, dried parsley, and balsamic vinegar.
2. Brush the vegetable skewers with the olive oil mixture and place them on a preheated 390°F (200°C) grill. Cook the kebabs for 3 minutes per side or until the vegetables are lightly browned.

Nutrition:

Calories: 88   Protein: 2.4 g   Sodium: 14 mg

Carbs: 13 g   Fat: 3.9 g   Potassium: 122mg

43. White Beans Stew

Preparation time: 15 minutes   Cooking time: 55 minutes   Servings: 4

Ingredients:

- 1/2 cup white beans, soaked
- 1/2 cup low-sodium vegetable broth
- 1/2 cup zucchini, chopped
- 1/2 tsp. tomato paste
- 1/2 tbsp. avocado oil
- 2 cups water
- 1/4 tsp. ground black pepper

Directions:

1. Heat avocado oil in a saucepan, add zucchinis, and roast them for 5 minutes. After this, add white beans, vegetable broth, tomato paste, water, and ground black pepper.
2. Simmer the stew for 50 minutes on low heat.

Nutrition:

Calories: 184   Carbs: 3.6 g   Sodium: 5 mg

Protein: 12.3 g   Fat: 1 g   Potassium: 142 mg

44. Vegetarian Lasagna

Preparation time: 15 minutes   Cooking time: 30 minutes   Servings: 2

Ingredients:

- 1/2 cup carrot, diced
- 1/4 cup bell pepper, diced
- 1/2 cup spinach, chopped
- 1/2 tbsp. olive oil

- 1/2 cup tomatoes, chopped
- 2 oz. low-fat cottage cheese
- 1/2 eggplant, sliced

Directions:
1. Put carrot, bell pepper, and spinach in a saucepan. Add olive oil and stir the vegetables well. Cook them for 5 minutes.
2. Make a sliced eggplant layer in a small casserole dish and top it with the vegetable mixture. Add tomatoes and cottage cheese. Bake the lasagna for 30 minutes at 375°F.

Nutrition:
Calories: 77 — Carbs: 9.7 g — Sodium: 24 mg
Protein: 4.1 g — Fat: 3 g — Potassium: 187mg

45. Pan-Fried Salmon with Salad

Preparation time: 15 minutes — Cooking time: 20 minutes — Servings: 2
Ingredients:
- Pinch of salt and pepper
- 1/2 tbsp. extra-virgin olive oil
- 1 tbsp. unsalted butter
- 1/4 tsp. fresh dill
- 1/2 tbsp. fresh lemon juice
- 50g salad leaves or a small bag of mixed leaves
- 1.5 tbsp. balsamic vinaigrette

Directions:
1. Pat-dry the salmon fillets with a paper towel and season with a pinch of salt and pepper. In a skillet, warm-up oil over medium-high heat and add fillets. Cook each side for 5 to 7 minutes until golden brown.
2. Melt butter, dill, and lemon juice in a small saucepan. Pour the butter mixture onto the cooked salmon. Drizzle balsamic vinaigrette onto the mixed salad leaves in a bowl and toss to coat. Serve the salmon with salad on the side.

Nutrition:
Calories: 307 — Fat: 22 g — Sodium: 80 mg
Carbs: 1.7 g — Protein: 34.6 g — Potassium: 192mg

46. Veggie Variety

Preparation time: 15 minutes — Cooking time: 15 minutes — Servings: 2
Ingredients:
- 1/2 onion, diced
- 1 tsp. vegetable oil (corn or sunflower oil)
- 200 g Tofu/bean curd
- 4 cherry tomatoes, halved
- 30ml vegetable milk (soy or oat milk)
- 1/2 tsp. curry powder
- 2 slices whole grain bread

Directions:
1. Dice the onion and fry in a frying pan with the oil. Break the tofu by hand into small pieces and put them in the pan. Sauté for 7-8 minutes.
2. Season with curry powder, salt, and pepper. Add the cherry tomatoes and milk, and cook for a few more minutes.
3. Serve with whole grain bread.

Nutrition:
Calories: 216 — Fat: 8.4 g — Sodium: 40 mg
Carbs: 24.8 g — Protein: 14.1 g — Potassium: 189mg

47. Vegetable Pasta

Preparation time: 15 minutes — Cooking time: 15 minutes — Servings: 2
Ingredients:
- 500 g thin zucchini
- 10 g fresh ginger
- 175 g tofu, smoked
- 1 lime
- 1 tbsp. sunflower oil
- 2 tbsp. sesame seeds
- Pinch salt and pepper

Directions:
1. Wash and clean the zucchini and, using a julienne cutter, cut the pulp around the kernel into long thin strips (noodles). Ginger peel and finely chop. Crumble tofu. Halve lime, squeeze juice.

2. Warm-up 1/2 tbsp. of oil in a pan and process the tofu for about 5 minutes. After about 3 minutes, add ginger, garlic, and sesame. Season with a pinch of salt and pepper. Remove from the pan and keep warm.
3. Wipe out the pan, then warm 1/2 tbsp. of oil in it. Stir fry zucchini strips for about 4 minutes while turning. Season with salt, pepper, and lime juice. Arrange pasta and tofu on plates.

Nutrition:

Calories: 262	Fat: 17.7 g	Sodium: 62 mg
Carbs: 7.1 g	Protein: 15.4 g	Potassium: 134mg

48. Vegetable Noodles with Bolognese

Preparation time: 15 minutes   Cooking time: 15 minutes   Servings: 2

Ingredients:

- 500 g small zucchini
- 300 g carrots
- 1/2 tbsp. olive oil
- 125 g beef steak
- Pinch salt and pepper
- 1 tbsp. tomato paste
- 20 g pecorino or parmesan cheese

Directions:

1. Clean and peel zucchini and carrots, then cut them into thin slices and then long, fine strips. Dice the beef steak.
2. Heat the olive oil in a large pan. Fry the beef steak until crumbly. Season with salt and pepper. Add the zucchini and carrot strips, and cook for a few minutes.
3. Stir in the tomato paste and add enough water to create a sauce-like consistency. Simmer for 7-8 minutes.
4. Shave the pecorino or parmesan cheese. Serve the vegetable noodles with bolognese, sprinkled with the cheese shavings.

Nutrition:

Calories: 269	Fat: 9.7 g	Sodium: 53 mg
Carbs: 1.7 g	Protein: 25.6 g	Potassium: 172 mg

49. Black Bean Burgers with Lettuce "Buns"

Preparation time: 20 minutes   Cooking time: 10 minutes   Servings: 2

Ingredients:

- 1/4 cup uncooked brown rice
- 1 1/2 cups canned low-sodium black beans, drained and rinsed
- 1/4 large red onion, chopped
- 1/2 large red bell pepper, diced
- 1/4 cup chopped fresh cilantro
- 1/2 teaspoon chili powder
- 1 head Boston lettuce

Directions:

1. Preheat the air fryer to 350F. Cook the brown rice according to package directions.
2. Mash the black beans in a large bowl, leaving some whole beans visible.
3. Stir in the brown rice, onion, bell pepper, cilantro, and chili powder until evenly combined. Transfer to the refrigerator for 5 minutes to chill, making it easier to form into patties.
4. Form the bean mixture into 2 patties, about 5 inches in diameter.
5. Place the burgers in a single layer in the air fryer basket and cook for 8 minutes. Flip them over and cook until golden brown.
6. To assemble, wrap 2 or 3 lettuce leaves tightly around each patty..

Nutrition:

Calories: 226	Protein: 18.6 g
Carbs: 13.8 g	Sodium: 19 mg
Fat: 11.2 g	Potassium: 87 mg

50. Curry Vegetable Noodles with Chicken

Preparation time: 15 minutes   Cooking time: 15 minutes   Servings: 2

Ingredients:

- 600g zucchini
- 500g chicken fillet
- Pinch salt and pepper
- 2 tbsp. oil

- 150 g red and yellow cherry tomatoes
- 1 tsp. curry powder
- 200 ml vegetable broth

Directions:

1. Wash the zucchini, clean, and cut into long thin strips with a spiral cutter. Wash the chicken, pat dry, and season with salt.
2. Heat oil in a pan. Cook the chicken for about 10 minutes until golden brown.
3. Wash cherry tomatoes and cut in half. Add the tomatoes to the chicken pan approximately 3 minutes before the end of the cooking time.
4. In another pan, heat the oil. Add curry powder, then stir in the vegetable broth. Season the sauce with salt and pepper and simmer for about 4 minutes.
5. Add the zucchini to the sauce and heat for 2-3 minutes.
6. Serve the vegetable noodles on plates, top with cooked chicken, and garnish with the cherry tomatoes.

Nutrition:

Calories: 376	Fat: 17.2 g	Sodium: 29 mg
Carbs: 9.5 g	Protein: 44.9 g	Potassium: 152 mg

51. Tempeh Veggie Tacos

Preparation time: 10 minutes	Cooking time: 10 minutes	Servings: 2

Ingredients:

- 6 ounces tempeh, cut into cubes
- 1/2 tablespoon chili powder
- 1/4 teaspoon ground cumin
- 1 tablespoon freshly squeezed lime juice
- 4 (6-inch) corn tortillas
- 1/2 cup chopped romaine lettuce
- 1/2 medium Hass avocado, sliced
- 1 jalapeño, sliced (optional)

Directions:

1. Preheat the air fryer to 325F.
2. In a medium bowl, stir together the tempeh, chili powder, cumin, and lime juice.
3. Working in batches if necessary, arrange the tempeh cubes in a single layer in the air fryer basket, ensuring not to crowd them. Cook for 10 minutes, or until the tempeh is browned and slightly crispy on the outside.
4. To assemble the tacos, layer the lettuce on the bottom of each tortilla. Top with the tempeh and avocado slices.

Nutrition:

Calories: 262	Carbs: 25g	Sodium: 42mg
Fat: 12.2g	Protein: 14g	Potassium: 88mg

52. Chickpea Frittata with Tomatoes and Watercress

Preparation time: 5 minutes	Cooking time: 10 minutes	Servings: 2

Ingredients:

- 1 cup chickpea flour
- 1 1/2 tablespoons nutritional yeast
- 1 cup filtered water
- 1/2 large bell pepper, chopped
- 6 ounces cherry tomatoes, chopped
- 1 cup chopped baby kale
- 1/2 cup watercress or pea shoots

Directions:

1. In a large bowl, whisk together the chickpea flour, nutritional yeast, and water until smooth. Stir in the bell pepper, tomatoes, and kale.
2. Working in batches if necessary, add the chickpea mixture to an air fryer baking pan, and smooth to an even layer. Place the pan in the air fryer basket and set the temperature to 375°F. Cook for 10 minutes, or until a toothpick inserted in the center comes out clean.
3. Top with the watercress or pea shoots and serve immediately.

Nutrition:

Calories: 269	Carbs: 21.7g	Sodium: 27mg
Fat: 4.9g	Protein: 12.8g	Potassium: 91mg

53. Harissa Bolognese with Vegetable Noodles

Preparation time: 15 minutes   Cooking time: 30 minutes   Servings: 2

Ingredients:

- 1 onion, finely diced
- 200g ground beef
- 1 tsp Harissa (Arabic seasoning paste)
- 1 sweet potato
- 1 medium zucchini
- 2-3 tbsp. oil
- 50g feta

Directions:

1. Warm-up 1 tbsp of oil in a wide saucepan. Fry the ground beef until crumbly. Add onion and cook until translucent. Stir in harissa.
2. Add 100ml of water to the pan, bring to the boil, and simmer for about 15 minutes with occasional stirring.
3. Peel the sweet potato and wash the zucchini. Cut the vegetables into spaghetti with a spiral cutter.
4. Warm-up 1-2 tablespoons of oil in a large pan. Cook sweet potato spaghetti for about 3 minutes. Add the zucchini spaghetti and continue to cook for 3-4 minutes, stirring occasionally.
5. Season the vegetable spaghetti with salt and pepper (optional). Serve the vegetable spaghetti and Bolognese on plates. Crumble feta over the top.

Nutrition:

Calories: 451   Carbs: 27.6g   Sodium: 7mg
Fat: 22.3g   Protein: 18.6g   Potassium: 96mg

54. Roasted Apple–Butternut Squash Soup

Preparation time: 20 minutes   Cooking time: 35 minutes   Servings: 2

Ingredients:

- 1 cup peeled and cubed butternut squash
- 1 cup peeled and cubed sweet potato
- 1/2 medium apple, cored and sliced into 1-inch cubes
- 1/2 teaspoon ground cinnamon
- Avocado oil cooking spray
- 1 3/4 cups low-sodium vegetable broth
- 1 small shallot, peeled and sliced

Directions:

1. Preheat the air fryer to 400°F.
2. Arrange the butternut squash, sweet potato, apple, and shallot in a single layer in the basket, being careful not to crowd them. Sprinkle with the cinnamon and mist with the avocado oil.
3. Cook the vegetables for 25 minutes, or until golden brown, shaking or stirring halfway through.
4. Carefully transfer the roasted vegetables to a 2-quart soup pot over medium heat. Add the broth and simmer for about 10 minutes.
5. Remove the soup from the heat and allow to cool slightly, then use an immersion blender or food processor to blend the vegetables until smooth.

Nutrition:

Calories: 376   Carbs: 9.5   Sodium: 32mg
Fat: 17.2g   Protein: 44.9g   Potassium: 119mg

55. Sweet and Sour Vegetable Noodles

Preparation time: 15 minutes   Cooking time: 30 minutes   Servings: 2

Ingredients:

- 2 chicken fillets (75 g each)
- 150g whole wheat spaghetti
- 375g carrots
- 1/4 liter low-sodium chicken broth
- 1/2 tablespoon sugar
- 1-2 tbsp. balsamic vinegar
- Pinch of salt

Directions:

1. Cook spaghetti in boiling water for about 8 minutes. Then drain. In the meantime, peel and wash carrots. Cut into long strips (best with a special grater). Set for 2 minutes in boiling salted water, drain. Wash chicken fillets. Add to the boiling chicken broth and cook for about 15 minutes.

2. Melt the sugar until golden brown. Measure 1/8 liter of low-sodium chicken broth and deglaze the sugar with it. Season with salt and vinegar. Add the fillets, then cut into thin slices. Turn the pasta and carrots in the sauce and serve.

Nutrition:

Calories: 374	Carbs: 23.1g	Sodium: 95 mg
Fat: 21g	Protein: 44g	Potassium: 133mg

56. Tuna Sandwich

Preparation time: 15 minutes   Cooking time: 0 minutes   Servings: 1

Ingredients:
- 2 slices whole grain bread
- 1 6-oz. can no-salt-added tuna in water
- 2 tsp. plain low-fat Greek yogurt
- 1 medium tomato, diced
- 1/2 small sweet onion, finely diced
- Lettuce leaves

Directions:
1. Toast whole grain bread slices. Drain the canned tuna and mix it with Greek yogurt, diced tomato, and onion in a bowl. Place lettuce leaves on one toasted bread slice.
2. Spread the tuna mixture over the lettuce leaves, and then place the other toasted bread slice on top to complete the sandwich.
3. Enjoy the sandwich.

Nutrition:

Calories: 235	Carbs: 25.9g	Sodium: 20mg
Fat: 3g	Protein: 27.8g	Potassium: 113mg

57. Sweet Potatoes and Zucchini Soup

Preparation time: 10 minutes   Cooking time: 20 minutes   Servings: 2

Ingredients:
- 1 cup low-sodium vegetable stock
- 1/2 tablespoon olive oil
- 1 small sweet potato, peeled and cubed
- 2 medium zucchinis, chopped
- 1/2 yellow onion, chopped
- 1/4 cup of light coconut milk
- A pinch of black pepper

Directions:
1. Heat a pot with olive oil over medium heat, add chopped onion, and cook for 5 minutes, stirring occasionally.
2. Add chopped zucchinis, cubed sweet potato, black pepper, and low-sodium vegetable stock to the pot. Stir and cook for 15 minutes more, or until the vegetables are tender.
3. Add the light coconut milk and use an immersion blender to blend the soup until smooth, or use a regular blender and carefully blend in batches.
4. Ladle the soup into bowls and serve immediately.

Nutrition:

Calories: 160	Fat: 6g	Sodium: 60 mg
Carbs: 19g	Protein: 4g	Potassium: 75mg

58. Lemongrass and Chicken Soup

Preparation time: 10 minutes   Cooking time: 25 minutes   Servings: 2

Ingredients:
- 2 cups low-sodium vegetable stock
- 1/2 lemongrass stalk, chopped
- 1/2 tablespoon ginger, grated
- 1/2 pound skinless, boneless chicken breast, cubed
- 4 ounces mushrooms, chopped
- 6.5 ounces of light coconut milk
- 2 tablespoons lime juice

Directions:
1. In a pot, bring the low-sodium vegetable stock to a simmer over medium heat. Add chopped lemongrass and grated ginger, and cook for 10 minutes. Strain the stock into another pot and heat it over medium heat again.
2. Add the cubed chicken, chopped mushrooms, light coconut milk, and lime juice to the pot. Stir and let it simmer for 15 minutes or until the chicken is cooked through.

3. Ladle the soup into bowls and serve immediately.

Nutrition:

Calories: 295	Fat: 13g	Sodium: 160mg
Carbs: 8g	Protein: 32g	Potassium: 90mg

59. Easy Lunch Salmon Steaks

Preparation time: 10 minutes   Cooking time: 20 minutes   Servings: 2

Ingredients:

- 1/2 large salmon fillet, cut into 2 steaks
- 1-2 garlic cloves, minced
- 1/2 yellow onion, chopped
- Black pepper to taste
- 1 tablespoon olive oil
- 2 tablespoons parsley, chopped
- Juice of 1/2 lemon

Directions:

1. Heat a pan with the olive oil on medium-high heat, and cook the chopped onion and minced garlic for 3 minutes.
2. Add black pepper, chopped parsley, and lemon juice to the pan. Stir and let the mixture cook for a minute.
3. Place the salmon steaks in the pan and cook for about 7-8 minutes per side, or until they are cooked through and flaky.
4. Divide the salmon steaks between two plates and serve with a side salad for lunch..

Nutrition:

Calories: 305	Fat: 14g	Sodium: 65 mg
Carbs: 4g	Protein: 38g	Potassium: 55 mg

60. Light Balsamic Salad

Preparation time: 10 minutes   Cooking time: 0 minutes   Servings: 2

Ingredients:

- 1 orange, cut into segments
- 1 green onion, chopped
- 1/2 Romaine lettuce head, torn
- 1/2 avocado, pitted, peeled, and cubed
- 2 tablespoons almonds, sliced

For the salad dressing:

- 2 tablespoons olive oil
- 1 tablespoon balsamic vinegar

Directions:

1. In a salad bowl, mix the orange segments with the avocado, lettuce, almonds, and chopped green onion.
2. In another bowl, whisk together the olive oil and balsamic vinegar. Drizzle this dressing over the salad and toss well.
3. Divide the salad between two plates and serve immediately..

Nutrition:

Calories: 266	Fat: 21g	Sodium: 14 mg
Carbs: 17g	Protein: 4g	Potassium: 664mg

61. Purple Potato Soup

Preparation time: 10 minutes   Cooking time: 1 hour and 15 minutes   Servings: 2

Ingredients:

- 2 purple potatoes, chopped
- 1/3 cauliflower head, florets separated
- 1 garlic clove, minced
- 1/2 yellow onion, chopped
- 1 tablespoon olive oil
- 2 cups low-sodium vegetable stock
- Black pepper to taste

Directions:

1. Preheat the oven to 400F. In a baking dish, mix the potatoes with onion, cauliflower, garlic, pepper, and olive oil. Toss to coat and bake for 45 minutes.
2. Heat a pot over medium-high heat, add the roasted vegetables and vegetable stock. Stir, bring to a boil, and cook for 20 minutes.
3. Carefully transfer the soup to a blender or use an immersion blender to blend until smooth. Divide the soup between two bowls and serve.

Nutrition:

Calories: 220	Fat: 7g	Sodium: 100 mg
Carbs: 35g	Protein: 6g	Potassium: 1030mg

62. Leeks Soup

Preparation time: 10 minutes	Cooking time: 45 minutes	Servings: 2

Ingredients:

- 1 gold potato, chopped
- 1/2 cup cauliflower florets
- 2 leeks, chopped
- 2 garlic cloves, minced
- 1/2 yellow onion, chopped
- 1 tablespoon olive oil
- 2 cups low-sodium vegetable stock
- Black pepper to taste

Directions:

1. Heat up a pot with the oil over medium-high heat, add onion and garlic, stir and cook for 5 minutes.
2. Add potatoes, cauliflower, black pepper, leeks, and vegetable stock, stir, bring to a simmer, and cook over medium heat for 30 minutes.
3. Use an immersion blender or carefully transfer the soup to a blender to blend until smooth. Ladle into bowls and serve.

Nutrition:

Calories: 225	Fat: 7g	Sodium: 120 mg
Carbs: 38g	Protein: 6g	Potassium: 960mg

63. Cauliflower Lunch Salad

Preparation time: 1 hour	Cooking time: 10 minutes	Servings: 2

Ingredients:

- 3 cups cauliflower florets, grated
- 1/8 cup low-sodium vegetable stock
- 1 tablespoon olive oil
- Black pepper to taste
- 1/4 red bell pepper, chopped
- Juice of 1/4 lemon
- 1/4 cup kalamata olives, halved

Directions:

1. Heat up a pan with the oil over medium-high heat, add cauliflower, black pepper, and vegetable stock, stir, and cook for 10 minutes. Transfer to a bowl and refrigerate for 1 hour.
2. Mix chilled cauliflower with olives, red bell pepper, and lemon juice. Toss to coat and serve.

Nutrition:

Calories: 205	Fat: 15g	Sodium: 110 mg
Carbs: 15g	Protein: 5g	Potassium: 660mg

64. Tofu and Green Bean Stir Fry

Preparation time: 15 minutes	Cooking time: 20 minutes	Servings: 2

Ingredients:

- 1/2 package (7 ounces) extra-firm tofu
- 1 tablespoon canola oil
- 1/2 pound green beans, chopped
- 1 carrot, peeled and thinly sliced
- 1/4 cup low-sodium stir fry sauce
- 1 cup cooked brown rice
- 1 tablespoon sesame seeds

Directions:

1. Press the tofu using a kitchen towel and a heavy pot to remove moisture for 15 minutes. Cut the tofu into 1-inch cubes.
2. Heat the canola oil in a large wok or skillet to medium-high heat. Add the tofu cubes and cook, flipping every 1 to 2 minutes, until all sides are browned. Remove from the skillet and add the green beans and carrots. Stir-fry for 4 to 5 minutes, occasionally tossing, until crisp and slightly tender.
3. Add the tofu back into the skillet. Pour the low-sodium stir fry sauce over the tofu and vegetables and let simmer for 2 to 3 minutes. Serve over brown rice and sprinkle with sesame seeds.

Nutrition:

Calories: 35	Sodium: 300mg	Carbohydrate: 35g
Fat: 15g	Potassium: 450mg	Protein: 15g

65. Spicy Tofu Burrito Bowls with Cilantro Avocado Sauce

Preparation time: 15 minutes   Cooking time: 15 minutes   Servings: 2

Ingredients:

For the sauce:

- 7-ounce package extra-firm tofu
- 1/2 tablespoon canola oil
- 1/2 yellow or orange bell pepper, diced
- 1 tablespoon taco seasoning (low-sodium)

- 1 cup fluffy brown rice
- 1/2 15-ounce can black beans, drained
- 1/4 ripe avocado, mashed

Directions:

1. Put the tofu on a plate lined with a kitchen towel. Place another kitchen towel over the tofu and put a heavy pot on top. Let it stand for 15 minutes to remove the moisture. Cut the tofu into 1-inch cubes.
2. Warm up the canola oil in a large skillet over medium heat. Add the tofu and bell pepper and sauté, breaking up the tofu into smaller pieces, for 4 to 5 minutes. Stir in the taco seasoning and 1/8 cup of water.
3. Evenly divide the rice and black beans between 2 bowls. Top with the tofu/bell pepper mixture and finish with a dollop of mashed avocado.

Nutrition:

Calories: 361   Carbs: 46 g   Protein: 20 g

Fat: 11g   Sodium: 138 mg   Potassium: 100 mg

66. Chickpea Cauliflower Tikka Masala

Preparation time: 15 minutes   Cooking time: 40 minutes   Servings: 2

Ingredients:

- 1 tablespoon olive oil
- 1/2 yellow onion, peeled and diced
- 1 garlic clove, peeled and minced
- 1 teaspoon garam masala
- 1/4 teaspoon ground cumin
- 1/4 teaspoon ground turmeric

- 1 15-ounce can of no-salt-added chickpeas, rinsed and drained
- 1/2 small head cauliflower, small florets
- 1 cup unsalted vegetable broth
- 1/2 15-ounce can coconut milk

Directions:

1. Warm up olive oil over medium heat in a Dutch oven or stockpot, then add the onion and sauté for 4 to 5 minutes.
2. Stir in the garlic, garam masala, cumin, and turmeric, and cook for another 30 seconds.
3. Add the cauliflower florets, chickpeas, and vegetable broth, and increase to medium-high heat. Simmer for 15 minutes, until the cauliflower is fork-tender.
4. Remove from heat, then stir in the coconut milk. Taste and adjust seasoning, if necessary. Serve with your choice of DASH diet-compliant side dish, such as brown rice or whole-grain flatbread.

Nutrition:

Calories: 328   Carbs: 32g   Protein: 11g

Fat: 19g   Sodium: 44 mg   Potassium: 80mg

67. Eggplant Parmesan Stacks

Preparation time: 15 minutes   Cooking time: 20 minutes   Servings: 4

Ingredients:

- 1/2 large eggplant, cut into thick slices
- 1 tablespoon olive oil
- 1/8 teaspoon salt
- 1/8 teaspoon ground black pepper

- 1/2 cup panko bread crumbs
- 1/8 cup freshly grated Parmesan cheese
- 1/4 pound fresh mozzarella, sliced

Directions:

1. Preheat the oven to 425°F. Coat the eggplant slices in olive oil and sprinkle with salt and black pepper. Place on a large baking sheet, then roast for 10 to 12 minutes, until soft with crispy edges. Remove the eggplant and set the oven to a low broil.

2. In a bowl, mix the panko bread crumbs and Parmesan cheese. Remove the cooled eggplant from the baking sheet and clean it.
3. Create layers on the same baking sheet by stacking a roasted eggplant slice with a slice of mozzarella, a tablespoon of the bread crumb mixture, and another eggplant slice. Place under the broiler for 3 to 4 minutes until the cheese is melted and bubbly.

Nutrition:

Calories: 378	Carbs: 29g	Protein: 18g
Fat: 22g	Sodium: 591mg	Potassium: 535mg

68. Tomato and Olive Orecchiette with Basil Pesto

Preparation time: 15 minutes   Cooking time: 25 minutes   Servings: 2

Ingredients:

- 4 ounces orecchiette pasta
- 1 tablespoon olive oil
- 1/3 pint cherry tomatoes, quartered
- 1/4 cup basil pesto or store-bought pesto
- 1/8 cup kalamata olives, sliced
- 1/4 teaspoon kosher or sea salt
- 1/8 teaspoon freshly cracked black pepper

Directions:

1. Boil a large pot of water. Cook the orecchiette, drain, and transfer the pasta to a large nonstick skillet.
2. Put the skillet over medium-low heat, then heat the olive oil. Stir in the cherry tomatoes, pesto, olives, salt, and black pepper. Cook for 8 to 10 minutes, until heated throughout. Serve the pasta immediately.

Nutrition:

Calories: 332	Carbs: 44g	Protein: 9g
Fat: 13g	Sodium: 389mg	Potassium: 129mg

69. Italian Stuffed Portobello Mushroom Burgers

Preparation time: 15 minutes   Cooking time: 25 minutes   Servings: 2

Ingredients:

- 1/2 tablespoon olive oil
- 2 large portobello mushrooms, washed and dried
- 1/4 yellow onion, peeled and diced
- 2 garlic cloves, peeled and minced
- 1/2 can cannellini beans, drained
- 1/4 cup panko bread crumbs
- 1/4 teaspoon kosher or sea salt

Directions:

1. Heat the olive oil in a large skillet to medium-high heat. Sear the mushrooms for 4 to 5 minutes per side, until slightly soft. Place on a baking sheet. Preheat the oven to a low broil.
2. Cook the onion in the skillet for 4 to 5 minutes, until slightly soft. Mix in the garlic then cook for 30 to 60 seconds. Move the onions and garlic to a bowl. Add the cannellini beans and smash with the back of a fork to form a chunky paste. Stir in the bread crumbs, salt, and cook for 5 minutes.
3. Remove the bean mixture from the stove and divide it among the mushroom caps. Broil for 4 minutes, until the filling is heated through. Transfer the burgers to your preferred serving dish or plate.

Nutrition:

Calories: 203	Carbs: 31.5g	Protein: 12.5g
Fat: 4.5g	Sodium: 75mg	Potassium: 61.45mg

70. French Toast Sticks with Yogurt-Berry Dipping Sauce

Preparation time: 10 minutes   Cooking time: 10 minutes   Servings: 2

Ingredients:

For the French toast sticks

- 1/2 large egg
- 1/2 cup unsweetened almond milk

For the sauce

- 1/2 cup blueberries

- 1 1/2 tablespoons ground cinnamon
- 2 slices whole-grain bread, each cut into 4 "sticks"

- 1 cup low-fat Greek yogurt

Directions:

To make the French toast sticks
1. Preheat the air fryer to 350F.
2. In a medium bowl, whisk together the egg, almond milk, and cinnamon.
3. Dip each piece of bread into the egg mixture, dredging it on all sides and making sure it is fully soaked.
4. Cooking in batches if necessary, place the pieces of bread in the air fryer basket in a single layer and cook for 5 minutes. Flip the sticks over and cook for another 3 minutes, or until golden brown.

To make the sauce
1. In a saucepan over medium-high heat, cook the blueberries for 4 minutes, or until the berries start to burst and release their juices. While still warm, pour the blueberries over the Greek yogurt and gently stir to combine.
2. To serve, dip the French toast sticks in the yogurt-berry sauce while warm.

Nutrition:

Calories: 195

Fat: 10g

Protein: 8g

Carbs: 19g

Sodium: 87 mg

Potassium: 112mg

11. Dinner

71. Apple Pie Crackers

Preparation time: 10 minutes Cooking time: 120 minutes Servings: 10 crackers

Ingredients:

- 2 tbsp. + 2 tsp. avocado oil
- 1 medium Granny Smith apple, roughly chopped
- 1/4 cup Erythritol
- 1/4 cup sunflower seeds, ground
- 1 3/4 cups flax seeds, roughly ground
- 1/8 tsp. cloves, ground
- 1/8 tsp. cardamom, ground
- 3 tbsp. nutmeg
- 1/4 tsp. ginger, ground

Directions:

1. Preheat your oven to 225F.
2. Set 2 baking sheets with parchment paper and keep them on the side.
3. Add oil, apple, Erythritol to a bowl and mix.
4. Transfer to a food processor and add remaining ingredients, process until combined.
5. Transfer batter to baking sheets, spread evenly, and cut into crackers.
6. Bake for 1 hour, flip and bake for another hour.
7. Let them cool and serve.
8. Enjoy!

Nutrition:

Calories: 70 Fat: 0g Sodium: 6 mg
Carbs: 1/5g Protein: 2g Potassium: 121.6mg

72. Orange and Chili Garlic Sauce

Preparation time: 15 minutes Cooking time: 8 hours Servings: 2

Ingredients:

- 1/8 cup apple cider vinegar
- 1 lb. red jalapeno peppers, stems, seeds, and ribs removed, chopped
- 5 garlic cloves, chopped
- 1/4 cup tomato paste
- Juice of 1/2 orange
- 1/4 cup honey
- 1 tbsp. low-sodium soy sauce

Directions:

1. Add apple cider vinegar, chopped jalapeno peppers, garlic, tomato paste, orange juice, honey, and low-sodium soy sauce to your slow cooker.
2. Stir and close the lid.
3. Cook on LOW for 8 hours.
4. Use as needed!

Nutrition:

Calories: 296 Fat: 1g Sodium: 277mg
Carbs: 68g Protein: 4.5g Potassium: 336mg

73. Tantalizing Mushroom Gravy

Preparation time: 5 minutes Cooking time: 5-8 hours Servings: 2

Ingredients:

- 1 cup button mushrooms, sliced
- 3/4 cup low-fat buttermilk
- 1/3 cup water
- 1 medium onion, finely diced
- 2 garlic cloves, minced
- 2 tbsp. extra virgin olive oil
- 1 tbsp. all-purpose flour

Directions:

1. Add the listed ingredients to your slow cooker.
2. Place the lid and cook on LOW for 5-8 hours.

3. Serve warm and use as needed!

Nutrition:

| Calories: 213 | Carbs: 14g | Sodium: 67mg |
| Fat: 16g | Protein: 5g | Potassium: 350mg |

74. Everyday Vegetable Stock

Preparation time: 5 minutes   Cooking time: 8-12 hours   Servings: 2

Ingredients:

- 1 celery stalk (with leaves), quartered
- 2 oz. mushrooms, with stems
- 1 carrot, unpeeled and quartered
- 1/2 onion, unpeeled, quartered from pole to pole
- 1/2 garlic head, unpeeled, halved across the middle
- 1 fresh thyme sprig
- Enough water to fill 3 quarters of the slow cooker

Directions:

1. Add celery, mushrooms, onion, carrot, garlic, thyme, and water to your slow cooker.
2. Stir and cover.
3. Cook on LOW for 8-12 hours.
4. Strain the stock through a fine-mesh cloth or metal mesh and discard solids.
5. Use as needed.

Nutrition:

| Calories: 19 | Carbs: 4g | Sodium: 25mg |
| Fat: 0g | Protein: 1g | Potassium: 240mg |

75. Grilled Chicken with Lemon and Fennel

Preparation time: 5 minutes   Cooking time: 25 minutes   Servings: 2

Ingredients:

- 1 cup chicken fillets, cut and skewed
- 1/2 large fennel bulb
- 1 garlic clove
- 1/4 cup green olives
- 1/2 lemon

Directions:

1. Preheat your grill to medium-high.
2. Crush the garlic clove.
3. In a bowl, mix a small amount of olive oil, crushed garlic, and a pinch of black pepper.
4. Coat chicken skewers with the marinade.
5. Grill the chicken skewers for 20 minutes, turning them halfway through until golden.
6. Zest half of the lemon and cut the other half into quarters.
7. Cut the fennel bulb into similarly sized segments.
8. Brush a small amount of olive oil all over the fennel segments and grill for 3-5 minutes.
9. In a bowl, mix the grilled fennel, lemon zest, and green olives.
10. Once the chicken is ready, serve with the vegetable mix.

Nutrition:

| Calories: 160 | Fat: 6g | Sodium: 74mg |
| Carbs: 4g | Protein: 20g | Potassium: 200mg |

76. Black Eyed Peas and Spinach Platter

Preparation time: 10 minutes   Cooking time: 8 hours   Servings: 2

Ingredients:

- 1/2 cup black-eyed peas, soaked overnight, and drained
- 1 cup low-sodium vegetable broth
- 1/2 can (7.5 oz.) tomatoes, diced with juice
- 4 oz. ham, chopped
- 1/2 onion, chopped
- 1 garlic clove, minced
- 1/2 tsp. dried oregano

Directions:
1. Add the listed ingredients to your Slow Cooker and stir.
2. Place lid and cook on LOW for 8 hours.
3. Serve and enjoy!

Nutrition:

Calories: 200

Protein: 14g

Carbs: 22g

Fat: 5g

Sodium: 150mg

Potassium: 400mg

77. Humble Mushroom Rice

Preparation time: 10 minutes   Cooking time: 3 hours   Servings: 2

Ingredients:

- 1/3 cup rice
- 1 green onion, chopped
- 1 garlic clove, minced
- 1/8 lb. baby Portobello mushrooms, sliced
- 2/3 cup low-sodium vegetable stock

Directions:
1. Add rice, green onion, garlic, mushrooms, and low-sodium vegetable stock to your Slow Cooker.
2. Stir well and place the lid.
3. Cook on LOW for 3 hours.
4. Stir and divide amongst serving platters.
5. Enjoy!

Nutrition:

Calories: 180

Carbs: 31g

Fat: 1.5g

Sodium: 100mg

Protein: 5g

Potassium: 180mg

78. Roasted Root Vegetables with Goat's Cheese Polenta

Preparation time: 35 minutes   Cooking time: 25 hours   Servings: 2

Ingredients:

Polenta:

- 2 cups low-sodium vegetable broth
- 1/2 cup polenta fine cornmeal/corn grits
- 1/4 cup goat's cheese
- 1 tbsp. extra-virgin olive oil
- 1/4 tsp. kosher salt
- 1/4 tsp. ground pepper

Vegetables:

- 1 tbsp. extra-virgin olive oil
- 1 clove garlic, smashed
- 2 cups roasted root vegetables
- 1 tbsp. torn fresh sage
- 1 tsp. low-sodium prepared pesto
- Fresh parsley for garnish (optional)

Directions:
1. To prepare the polenta: Bring the low-sodium vegetable broth to a boil in a medium saucepan. Set the heat to low and gradually add the polenta whisking vigorously to avoid clumping. Cook and stir for 10 minutes. Stir, and continue cooking until thickened and creamy. Stir in the goat's cheese, olive oil, salt, and pepper.
2. Meanwhile, to prepare the vegetables: Heat the olive oil in a medium skillet over medium heat. Add the garlic and cook, stirring, until fragrant, about 1 minute. Add the roasted root vegetables and cook, stirring often, until heated through, 2 to 4 minutes. Stir in the torn sage and cook until fragrant, about 1 minute more.
3. Serving Suggestion: Serve the vegetables over the polenta, topped with the low-sodium pesto. Garnish with parsley, if desired.

Nutrition:

Calories: 380

Carbs: 38 g

Fat: 19 g

Protein: 11 g

Sodium: 240 mg

Potassium: 530 mg

79. Fish Stew

Preparation time: 10 minutes   Cooking time: 30 minutes   Servings: 2

Ingredients:

- 1/2 red onion, sliced
- 1 tbsp. olive oil
- 1/2 lb. white fish fillets, boneless, skinless, and cubed
- 1/2 cup low-sodium chicken or vegetable stock
- 1 tomato, cubed
- 1/4 tsp. black pepper
- 1 tbsp. parsley, chopped

Directions:

1. Warm up the oil in a pot over medium heat, add the onion, and sauté for 5 minutes.
2. Add the fish, stock, tomato, and black pepper to the pot, stir, and cook over medium heat for 25 minutes.
3. Divide into bowls, garnish with chopped parsley, and serve.

Nutrition:

Calories: 230   Fat: 9 g   Sodium: 100 mg
Carbs: 6 g   Protein: 30 g   Potassium: 620 mg

80. Gnocchi Pomodoro

Preparation Time: 35 minutes   Cooking Time: 35 minutes   Servings: 2

Ingredients

- 1 1/2 tbsp. extra-virgin olive oil
- 1/2 medium onion, finely chopped
- 1 large clove garlic, minced
- 3/4 cup no-salt-added whole tomatoes, pulsed in a food processor until chunky
- 1/8 tsp. salt
- 1/2 tbsp. chopped fresh basil
- 1/2 (17.5 oz.) package shelf-stable gnocchi or (6 oz.) package frozen cauliflower gnocchi

Directions:

1. Heat 1 tbsp. of the oil in a skillet. Add the onion and cook, stirring, until softened, for about 5 minutes.
2. Add the garlic and cook until softened for about 1 minute.
3. Add the tomatoes and salt and bring to a simmer. Lower the heat to maintain the simmer and cook, stirring often, until thickened (about 20 minutes).
4. Remove from the heat and stir in the basil.
5. Meanwhile, heat the remaining 1/2 tbsp. of oil in a non-stick skillet. Add the gnocchi and cook, stirring often, until plumped and starting to brown (5 to 7 minutes). Add the gnocchi to the tomato sauce and stir until coated.

Nutrition:

Calories: 367   Carbs: 53 g   Sodium: 200 mg
Protein: 5 g   Fat: 14 g   Potassium: 305 mg

81. Slow-Cooked Pasta e Fagioli Soup

Preparation time: 8 hours 15 minutes   Cooking Time: 15 minutes   Servings: 6

Ingredients

- 2 1 cup chopped onions
- 1/2 cup chopped carrots
- 1/2 cup chopped celery
- 8 oz. pre-cooked chicken thighs, diced
- 2 cups cooked whole-wheat rotini pasta
- 3 cups reduced-sodium chicken broth
- 15 oz. /1/2 can no-salt-added white beans, rinsed

Directions:

1. In a large pot or slow cooker, add the onions, carrots, and celery.
2. Add the chicken, cooked pasta, chicken broth, and white beans.
3. Cook on low heat for about 2 hours, stirring occasionally.
4. Taste and adjust seasoning as needed. If desired, you may add salt, pepper, or Italian seasoning.
5. Serve hot, and enjoy!

Nutrition:

Calories: 710   Carbohydrates: 86 g   Sodium: 400 mg
Protein: 55 g   Fat: 15 g   Potassium: 700 mg

82. Salmon Couscous Salad

Preparation time: 10 minutes　　　　Cooking time: 10 minutes　　　　Servings: 1

Ingredients

- 1/4 cup sliced cremini mushrooms
- 1/4 cup diced eggplant
- 3 cups baby spinach
- 1 tbsp. white-wine vinaigrette or lemon juice
- 1/4 cup cooked whole-wheat couscous
- 4 oz. cooked salmon
- 1/4 cup sliced dried apricots

Directions:

1. Heat a small non-stick skillet over medium-high heat. Add the mushrooms and eggplant. Cook, stirring occasionally, until lightly browned and the juices have been released (about 3 to 5 minutes). Remove from heat and set aside.
2. Toss the spinach with the white-wine vinaigrette or lemon juice.
3. On a plate, layer the spinach, cooked whole-wheat couscous, cooked vegetables, cooked salmon, and sliced dried apricots.

Nutrition:

Calories: 480　　　　Carbohydrates: 54 g　　　　Sodium: 220 mg
Protein: 36 g　　　　Fat: 15 g　　　　Potassium: 1000 mg

83. Roasted Salmon with Smoky Chickpeas and Greens

Preparation time: 40 minutes　　　　Cooking time: 40 minutes　　　　Servings: 2

Ingredients

- 1 tbsp. extra-virgin olive oil
- 1/2 tbsp. smoked paprika
- 1 (15 oz.) can no-salt-added chickpeas, rinsed and drained
- 5 cups chopped kale
- 1/4 cup water
- 2 salmon fillets (about 10 oz. total)
- Salt and pepper, to taste

Directions:

1. Preheat oven to 425°F (220°C).
2. In a medium bowl, combine 1/2 tbsp. of olive oil, smoked paprika, and a pinch of salt. Thoroughly pat the chickpeas dry, then toss with the paprika mixture.
3. Spread the chickpea mixture on a baking sheet. Bake on the middle rack, stirring occasionally, for 30 minutes.
4. Meanwhile, heat the remaining 1/2 tbsp. of olive oil in a skillet over medium heat. Add the kale and cook, stirring occasionally, for 2 minutes.
5. Add the water to the skillet and continue cooking until the kale is tender, about 5 minutes more. Season with salt and pepper to taste. Remove from heat and keep warm.
6. Remove the chickpeas from the oven and push them to one side of the pan. Place the salmon fillets on the other side and season with salt and pepper. Bake until the salmon is just cooked through, about 5 to 8 minutes.
7. Serve the salmon alongside the chickpeas and sautéed kale.

Nutrition:

Calories: 595　　　　Carbohydrates: 45 g　　　　Sodium: 160 mg
Protein: 48 g　　　　Fat: 27 g　　　　Potassium: 1100 mg

84. Salmon with Salsa

Preparation time: 10 minutes　　　　Cooking time: 8 minutes　　　　Servings: 1

Ingredients:

For Salsa:

- 1/2 cup fresh pineapple, chopped
- 1/4 cup red bell pepper, seedless and chopped
- 1 tbsp. red onion, chopped
- 1/2 tbsp. fresh lemon juice

For Salmon:

- 1 salmon fillet
- 1/2 tbsp. extra-virgin olive oil
- Salt and fresh ground black pepper, to taste

Directions:

For Salsa:

1. In a bowl, combine pineapple, red bell pepper, red onion, and lemon juice.
2. Refrigerate until ready to serve.

For Salmon:

1. Season the salmon with salt and black pepper.
2. In a frying pan, heat the olive oil over medium-high heat.
3. Add the salmon fillet, skin side up, and cook for about 4 minutes.
4. Carefully flip the fillet and cook for about 4 more minutes, or until cooked to your desired level.
5. Serve the salmon with a generous spoonful of pineapple salsa on top or alongside it.

Nutrition:

Calories: 325   Carbohydrates: 10 g   Sodium: 110 mg

Fat: 17 g   Protein: 35 g   Potassium: 440 mg

85. Bruschetta Chicken

Preparation time: 8 minutes   Cooking time: 12 minutes   Servings: 2

Ingredients:

For Chicken:

- 2 boneless, skinless chicken breasts, halved horizontally
- 1 1/2 tsp. salt-free Italian seasoning
- 1/2 tbsp. olive oil
- 1 tsp. garlic, minced

For Topping:

- 1 1/2 garlic cloves, chopped finely
- 2 Roma tomatoes, chopped finely
- 2 tbsp. fresh basil, shredded
- 1 tbsp. olive oil

Directions:

For Chicken:

1. In a bowl, mix the chicken, garlic, and Italian seasoning.
2. Heat olive oil in a frying pan over medium-high heat and cook the chicken breasts for about 6 minutes per side or until cooked through and browned.

Topping:

1. In a separate bowl, combine garlic, tomatoes, fresh basil, and olive oil.
2. Remove the frying pan from the heat and let the chicken rest for a few minutes.
3. Top each chicken breast with the tomato mixture and serve immediately.

Nutrition:

Calories: 275   Carbs: 6 g   Sodium: 100 mg

Fat: 15 g   Protein: 29 g   Potassium: 360 mg

86. Quinoa Power Salad

Preparation time: 15 minutes   Cooking time: 25 minutes   Servings: 2

Ingredients

- 1 medium sweet potato, skinned and cut into 1/2-inch thick wedges
- 1/2 red onion, cut into 1/4-inch thick wedges
- 2 tbsp. extra-virgin olive oil, divided
- 1/2 tsp. garlic powder
- 8 oz. chicken tender
- 4 cups mixed greens (kale, spinach, or arugula)
- 1/2 cup cooked red quinoa, cooled

Directions:

1. Preheat the oven to 425°F. In a medium bowl, mix the sweet potato and onion with 1 tbsp. of oil and garlic powder.
2. Spread the mixture on a large rimmed baking sheet and roast for 15 minutes.
3. Meanwhile, coat the chicken with the remaining 1 tbsp. of oil.
4. After the vegetables have roasted for 15 minutes, remove them from the oven and stir. Add the chicken to the baking sheet and return to the oven. Continue roasting until the vegetables begin to brown and the chicken is cooked through (about 10 minutes more). Remove from the oven and let cool.
5. In a large bowl, combine the roasted vegetables, chicken, mixed greens, and cooked quinoa. Toss to mix and serve.

Nutrition:

Calories: 430	Carbs: 42 g	Sodium: 120 mg
Protein: 31 g	Fat: 15 g	Potassium: 450 mg

87. Balsamic Roast Chicken Breast

Preparation time: 10 minutes   Cooking time: 35 minutes   Servings: 2

Ingredients:

- 2 skinless chicken breasts (4 ounces each)
- Black pepper to taste
- 1 teaspoon finely chopped fresh garlic
- 1 tablespoon fresh thyme, chopped
- 1/2 cup balsamic vinegar
- 8 ounces broccoli florets
- 2 tablespoons toasted cashew nuts (optional)

Directions:

1. Preheat the oven to 375°F (190°C).
2. In a small pot, bring 1/2 cup balsamic vinegar, garlic, pepper, and thyme to a boil. Simmer for about 3 minutes, or until the liquid has reduced by about half. Let the mixture cool for 5 minutes.
3. Grease a baking tray and place the chicken breasts on it. Cover the chicken with the cooled marinade and let it marinate for 30 minutes.
4. In a bowl, mix the broccoli florets with some black pepper.
5. Grease a second baking tray and spread the broccoli on it. After 30 minutes, cover the marinated chicken with foil and place it in the oven to roast for 30-35 minutes.
6. For the last 15-20 minutes, place the broccoli in the oven to roast as well. Stir the broccoli at least once while cooking.
7. Once the chicken is cooked, serve it hot with the roasted broccoli on the side. If desired, garnish with toasted cashew nuts.

Nutrition:

Calories: 295	Sodium: 85mg	Protein: 36g
Fat: 9g	Carbs: 16g	Potassium: 560mg

88. Stuffed Eggplant Shells

Preparation time: 15 minutes   Cooking time: 25 minutes   Servings: 2

Ingredients:

- 1 medium eggplant
- 1 tablespoon olive oil
- 4 ounces cooked white beans
- 1/4 cup onion, chopped
- 1 cup canned unsalted tomatoes
- 1 cup fresh mushrooms, sliced
- 3/4 cup whole-wheat breadcrumbs

Directions:

1. Preheat the oven to 350°F (180°C).
2. Grease a baking dish with cooking spray and set it aside.
3. Trim and cut the eggplant in half, lengthwise.
4. Scoop out the pulp using a spoon, leaving the shell about 1/4-inch thick.
5. Place the shells in the baking dish with their cut side up.
6. Dice the eggplant pulp into cubes and set them aside.
7. Add oil to a skillet and heat it over medium heat.
8. Stir in the onions, chopped eggplant pulp, tomatoes, and mushrooms.
9. Cook for 10 minutes on simmering heat, then stir in the beans and breadcrumbs.
10. Divide this mixture into the eggplant shells.
11. Cover the shells with a foil sheet and bake for 15 minutes.
12. Serve warm.

Nutrition:

Calories: 350	Sodium: 85mg	Protein: 13g
Fat: 12g	Carbs: 48g	Potassium: 600mg

89. Zucchini Pepper Kebabs

Preparation time: 15 minutes   Cooking time: 20 minutes   Servings: 4

Ingredients:

- 1 small zucchini, sliced into 4 pieces
- 1/2 red onion, cut into 2 wedges
- 1/2 green bell pepper, cut into 2 chunks
- 4 cherry tomatoes
- 4 button mushrooms
- 1/4 cup fat-free Italian dressing
- 1/4 cup brown rice

Directions:

1. In a bowl, toss the zucchini, onion, green bell pepper, cherry tomatoes, and mushrooms with the Italian dressing. Mix well to coat the vegetables and marinate for 10 minutes.
2. Cook the brown rice according to package instructions.
3. Preheat the broiler on medium heat.
4. Grease the broiler rack with cooking spray and place it 4 inches below the heat source.
5. Assemble 2 skewers, each with 2 mushroom pieces, 2 tomatoes, 2 zucchini slices, 1 onion wedge, and 1 green pepper slice.
6. Broil the kebabs for about 5-7 minutes per side or until the vegetables are tender and slightly charred.
7. Serve warm alongside the cooked brown rice.

Nutrition:

Calories: 376   Sodium: 76mg   Protein: 10g
Fat: 11g   Carbs: 67g   Potassium: 198mg

90. Corn Stuffed Peppers

Preparation time: 15 minutes   Cooking time: 25 minutes   Servings: 2

Ingredients:

- 2 red or green bell peppers
- 1/2 tablespoon olive oil
- 1/8 cup onion, chopped
- 1 1/4 cups fresh corn kernels
- 1/16 teaspoon chili powder
- 1 1/2 tablespoons parsley, chopped
- 1/4 cup skim milk

Directions:

1. Preheat the oven to 350F.
2. Grease a baking dish with cooking spray.
3. Cut the bell peppers from the top and remove their seeds.
4. Place the peppers in the baking dish with their cut side up.
5. Add the oil to a skillet, then heat it on medium flame.
6. Stir in the onion, corn, and chopped green pepper. Sauté for 5 minutes.
7. Add the parsley and chili powder. Switch the heat to low.
8. Whisk the milk in a bowl.
9. Pour the milk into the skillet and cook for 5 minutes while stirring.
10. Divide this mixture into each pepper.
11. Add some water to the baking dish.
12. Cover the stuffed peppers with an aluminum sheet.
13. Bake for 15 minutes, then serve warm.

Nutrition:

Calories: 250   Carbs: 40g   Protein: 7g
Fat: 8g   Sodium: 40mg   Potassium: 350mg

91. South Asian Baked salmon

Preparation time: 15 minutes   Cooking time: 20 minutes   Servings: 2

Ingredients:

- 1/2 cup sugar-free pineapple juice
- 1 garlic clove, minced
- 1/4 teaspoon ground ginger
- 2 salmon fillets
- 1/4 teaspoon sesame oil
- Ground black pepper, to taste

- 1/2 cup diced fresh fruit, as desired (such as pineapple or mango)

Directions:

1. Mix the pineapple juice with the garlic and ginger in a bowl.
2. Place the fish in a baking dish.
3. Pour the pineapple mixture over the fish and marinate in the refrigerator for 1 hour, gently flipping the fish halfway through.
4. Meanwhile, preheat the oven to 375°F.
5. Spread out two squares of aluminum foil and layer them with cooking spray.
6. Place the salmon fillets on each square.
7. Top the fish with the sesame oil, pepper, and diced fruit.
8. Fold the aluminum sheets to seal the fish and place them on a baking sheet.
9. Bake for 20 minutes, turning the parcels halfway through.
10. Serve warm.

Nutrition:

Calories: 245	Sodium: 75mg	Protein: 23g
Fat: 16g	Carbs: 6g	Potassium: 112mg

92. Sweet Potato Carbonara with Spinach and Mushrooms

Preparation time: 40 minutes Cooking time: 20 minutes Servings: 2

Ingredients:

- 1 lb. sweet potatoes, peeled
- 1 large egg, beaten
- 1/2 cup grated parmesan cheese
- 1/8 tsp. ground pepper
- 1/2 tbsp. extra-virgin olive oil
- 4 oz. sliced mushrooms
- 2.5 oz. baby spinach

Directions:

1. Bring a pot of water to boil.
2. Cut the sweet potatoes lengthwise into long, thin strands using a spiral vegetable slicer or julienne vegetable peeler.
3. Cook the sweet potatoes in the boiling water, gently stirring once or twice, until just starting to soften but not completely crisp (around 1 1/2 to 3 minutes). Reserve 1/8 cup of the cooking water, then drain. Return the noodles to the pot, off the heat.
4. Combine the egg, parmesan, pepper, and the reserved water in a bowl. Pour the mixture over the noodles and gently toss with tongs until evenly coated.
5. Heat the oil in a large skillet over medium heat. Add the mushrooms and cook, stirring often, until the liquid has evaporated and the mushrooms are starting to brown (around 6 to 8 minutes).
6. Add the spinach and cook, stirring, until wilted, for 1 to 2 minutes. Add the vegetables to the noodles and toss to combine.

Nutrition:

Calories: 315	Carbs: 37g	Sodium: 350mg
Protein: 15g	Fat: 12g	Potassium: 850mg

93. Hazelnut-Parsley Roast Tilapia

Preparation time: 30 minutes Cooking time: 20 minutes Servings: 2

Ingredients:

- 1 tbsp. olive oil
- 2 (5 oz.) tilapia fillets (fresh or frozen, thawed)
- 3 tbsp. finely chopped hazelnuts
- 2 tbsp. finely chopped fresh parsley
- 1 tsp. lemon zest
- 1/8 tsp. salt
- 1/8 tsp. ground pepper

Directions:

1. Preheat the oven to 450F. Line a large rimmed baking sheet with foil and brush with 1/2 tbsp. of oil.
2. Bring the fish to room temperature by leaving it on the counter for 15 minutes.
3. Meanwhile, stir together the hazelnuts, parsley, lemon zest, 1/2 tsp. of oil, salt, and pepper in a small bowl.

4. Pat both sides of the fish dry with a paper towel. Place the fish on the prepared baking sheet. Drizzle both sides of the fish with the remaining 1/2 tsp. of oil.
5. Press the hazelnut mixture evenly onto the tops of the fillets and pat gently to adhere.
6. Bake the fish until it is opaque, firm, and just beginning to flake (7 to 10 minutes).

Nutrition:

Calories: 280	Carbs: 3g	Sodium: 190mg
Protein: 30g	Fat: 17g	Potassium: 520mg

94. Fig and Goat's Cheese Salad

Preparation time: 10 minutes   Cooking time: 10 minutes   Servings: 1

Ingredients:

- 2 cups mixed salad greens
- 4 dried figs, stemmed and sliced
- 1 oz. fresh goat's cheese, crumbled
- 1 1/2 tbsp. slivered almonds, preferably toasted
- 2 tsp. extra-virgin olive oil
- 2 tsp. balsamic vinegar
- Freshly ground pepper to taste

Directions:
1. Combine the greens, figs, goat's cheese, and almonds in a medium bowl.
2. Stir together the oil, vinegar, and pepper. Drizzle the dressing over the salad and toss gently to combine.

Nutrition:

Calories: 320	Carbs: 33g	Sodium: 150mg
Protein: 10g	Fat: 18g	Potassium: 580mg

95. Masala Chickpeas

Preparation time: 10 minutes   Cooking time: 25 minutes   Servings: 2

Ingredients:

- 1 1/2 teaspoon garam masala powder
- 1 teaspoon ground cumin (jeera powder)
- 1 teaspoon ground coriander
- 1/2 tablespoon canola oil
- 1/2 white onion, diced
- 2 tablespoons finely chopped garlic
- 1 large sweet red pepper, diced
- 15 ounces cooked chickpeas, rinsed and drained
- 1/2 tablespoon tomato paste
- 5 ounces frozen kale, thawed

Directions:
1. In a small bowl, make the spice blend by mixing garam masala, ground cumin, and ground coriander. Set aside.
2. Heat the oil in a medium pot, then add in the diced onion and garlic. Sauté for 3 minutes.
3. Add the red pepper and cook on medium heat for about 3 minutes.
4. Stir in the spice blend and cook for an additional 2 minutes, allowing the spices to release their aroma.
5. Add the chickpeas, tomato paste, and kale to the pot. Stir well to combine.
6. Add enough water to cover the ingredients and bring to a slow boil. Cook for about 15-20 minutes or until the vegetables are cooked through and the stew smells aromatic.
7. Enjoy.

Nutrition:

Calories: 350	Sodium: 200mg	Protein: 17g
Fat: 8g	Carbs: 55g	Potassium: 950mg

96. Orecchiette with Broccoli Rabe

Preparation time: 30 minutes   Cooking time: 15 minutes   Servings: 2

Ingredients:

- 1/8 tsp. salt
- 6 oz. orecchiette pasta (about 1 3/4 cups)
- 1 lb. broccoli rabe
- 2 tbsp. extra-virgin olive oil
- 1 clove garlic, chopped
- 1/4 tsp. crushed red pepper
- 1/2 pint cherry tomatoes, halved

Directions:

1. Set 1 quart of water to boil in a large pot. Stir in salt, add the pasta, and cook until just tender. Drain, set aside 1/4 cup of the water.
2. Meanwhile, thoroughly wash the broccoli rabe and trim off the tough ends. Chop the rabe into 2-inch lengths. Leave some water clinging to the leaves and stems (this will help create a sauce).
3. Heat the oil in a large skillet over medium heat until it starts to shimmer. Add the garlic and crushed red pepper, and cook for about 1 minute.
4. Add the broccoli rabe. Cook, stirring, until almost tender (6 to 10 minutes).
5. Add the tomatoes and toss until they begin to soften (about 2 minutes).
6. Add the pasta and toss to coat. If it's too dry, add a little of the reserved pasta water.

Nutrition:

Calories: 390	Carbs: 60g	Sodium: 250mg
Protein: 15g	Fat: 13g	Potassium: 600mg

97. Chicken and Strawberry Salad

Preparation time: 10 minutes   Cooking time: 16 minutes   Servings:2

Ingredients:

- 2 tbsp. olive oil
- 2 tbsp. lemon juice
- 1/2 pound boneless, skinless chicken breasts
- 1 cup fresh strawberries, halved
- 1 small garlic clove, minced
- 2 cups fresh spinach, torn
- 1/8 tsp. salt

Directions:

1. For marinade: Take a bowl and add oil, lemon juice, garlic, salt and mix them well until well combined.
2. In a large resealable plastic bag, place the chicken and half of the marinade.
3. Secure the bag and shake it to coat well. Refrigerate for at least 1 hour.
4. Preheat the grill to medium heat.
5. Grease the grill grate finely.
6. Remove the chicken from the bag and discard the marinade.
7. Place the chicken onto the grill grate and grill it covered for about five to eight minutes per side. Remove chicken from the grill and cut into small pieces.
8. In a large bowl, add the chicken pieces, strawberries, and spinach. Add the reserved marinade and toss to coat well.
9. Serve immediately and enjoy!

Nutrition:

Calories: 370	Carbs: 10g	Sodium: 300mg
Fat: 23g	Protein: 30g	Potassium: 700mg

98. Mixed Vegetable Salad with Lime Dressing

Preparation time: 15 minutes   Cooking time: 15 minutes   Servings: 2

Ingredients:

- 2 tbsp. extra-virgin olive oil
- 1 1/2 tbsp. lime juice
- 1/8 tsp. salt
- 1/2 tsp. ground pepper
- 1 cup mixed vegetables, steamed (carrots, green beans, peas) and raw (cucumbers, tomatoes)
- 2 leaves romaine or leaf lettuce
- 1/4 cup crumbled feta cheese

Directions:

1. Whisk the olive oil, lime juice, salt, and pepper in a medium bowl until thoroughly blended.
2. Add the mixed vegetables and toss to coat.
3. Serve the salad over the lettuce leaves and garnish with feta cheese.

Nutrition:

Calories: 232	Carbs: 9g	Sodium: 340mg
Protein: 3g	Fat: 21g	Potassium: 300mg

99. Spinach Ginger Lentils

Preparation time: 10 minutes   Cooking time: 16 minutes   Servings: 2

Ingredients:

- 1/2 tbsp. olive oil
- 1/2 tsp. ground ginger
- 1/4 tsp. curry powder
- 1/2 cup yellow lentils, drained
- 3/4 cup vegetable stock
- 1 cup baby spinach leaves, chopped
- 1/4 tsp. salt

Directions:

1. Add the olive oil to a saucepan, then heat it over medium flame.
2. Stir in the ginger, curry powder, and lentils.
3. Add the stock and let the lentils boil, then reduce the heat to a simmer.
4. Partially cover the pan, then cook for 12 minutes.
5. Add the spinach to the lentils and cook for 3 minutes.
6. Adjust the seasoning with salt.
7. Serve warm.

Nutrition:

Calories: 220   Carbs: 33g   Sodium: 300mg
Fat: 4g   Protein: 15g   Potassium: 450mg

100.   Basil Halibut

Preparation time: 10 minutes   Cooking time: 20 minutes   Servings: 2

Ingredients:

- 2 halibut fillets, 4 ounces each
- 1 tsp. olive oil
- 1/2 tbsp. garlic, minced
- 1 tomato, diced
- 1 tbsp. basil, fresh and chopped
- 1/2 tsp. oregano, fresh and chopped

Directions:

1. Heat the oven to 350°F and prepare a 9 by 13-inch pan by spraying it with cooking spray.
2. Mix the basil, olive oil, garlic, oregano, and tomato in a bowl. Pour this over the fish in the pan.
3. Bake for 12 minutes or until the fish flakes easily with a fork.

Nutrition:

Calories: 200   Fat: 9g   Sodium: 100mg
Protein: 24g   Carbs: 5g   Potassium: 600mg

101.   Leek and Cauliflower Soup

Preparation time: 10 minutes   Cooking time: 20 minutes   Servings: 2

Ingredients:

- 1/2 tablespoon olive oil
- 1/2 leek, trimmed and sliced thin
- 1/2 head cauliflower, chopped into florets
- 1 clove garlic, minced
- 1 tablespoon fresh thyme, chopped
- 1 1/2 cups unsalted vegetable stock
- 1/4 teaspoon sea salt

Directions:

1. Heat oil in a pot over medium heat, and add leek, cauliflower, and garlic. Cook for 5 minutes until the leek begins to soften. Add thyme, salt, and vegetable stock, then bring to a simmer. Cook for 15 minutes or until cauliflower is tender.
2. Remove from heat and use an immersion blender to puree the soup. Serve warm.

Nutrition:

Calories: 110   Fat: 5g   Sodium: 250mg
Protein: 5g   Carbs: 14g   Potassium: 450mg

102.   Sweet and Sour Cabbage and Apples

Preparation time: 10 minutes   Cooking time: 8 hours   Servings: 2

Ingredients:

- 2 tablespoons honey
- 2 tablespoons apple cider vinegar
- 1/4 teaspoon sea salt
- 1 sweet-tart apple, peeled, cored, and sliced
- 1/2 head green cabbage, cored and shredded
- 1/4 sweet red onion, thinly sliced

Directions:

1. In a small bowl, whisk honey, vinegar, and salt.
2. Add honey mixture, apples, onion, and cabbage to a slow cooker and stir.
3. Cook on low for 8 hours.
4. Serve and enjoy!

Nutrition:

Calories: 180   Carbs: 44g   Sodium: 200mg

Fat: 1g   Protein: 4g   Potassium: 450mg

103.   Delicious Aloo Palak

Preparation time: 10 minutes   Cooking time: 6-8 hours   Servings: 2

Ingredients:

- 1 pound red potatoes, chopped
- 1/4 small onion, diced
- 1/4 red bell pepper, seeded and diced
- 2 tablespoons fresh cilantro, chopped
- 1/4 cup low-sodium veggie broth
- 1/4 teaspoon salt
- 1 pound fresh spinach, chopped

Directions:

1. Add potatoes, bell pepper, onion, cilantro, broth, and salt to your slow cooker. Mix well.
2. Add spinach on top.
3. Place the lid and cook on LOW for 6-8 hours.
4. Stir and serve.

Nutrition:

Calories: 280   Carbs: 58g   Sodium: 400mg

Fat: 1g   Protein: 12g   Potassium: 2100mg

104.   Hasselback Eggplant Parmesan

Preparation time: 1 hour 10 minutes   Cooking time: 25 minutes   Servings: 2

Ingredients:

- 1 cup low-sodium marinara sauce
- 2 small eggplants (about 6 inches long)
- 2 tbsp. extra-virgin olive oil, divided
- 2 oz. fresh mozzarella, thinly sliced
- 1/4 cup whole-wheat panko breadcrumbs
- 2 tbsp. grated parmesan cheese
- 1 tbsp. chopped fresh basil

Directions:

1. Preheat the oven to 375F.
2. Spread the marinara sauce in a 9 x 13-inch baking dish.
3. Make crosswise cuts every 1/4 inch along each eggplant, slicing almost to the bottom but not all the way through.
4. Gently transfer the eggplants to the baking dish. Gently fan them to open the cuts wider. Drizzle 1 tbsp. of oil over the eggplants. Insert mozzarella slices into the cuts. Cover with foil.
5. Bake until the eggplants are very tender, 45 to 55 minutes.
6. Combine the panko, parmesan, and the remaining oil in a small bowl. Remove the foil and sprinkle the eggplants with the breadcrumb mixture.
7. Change the oven setting to broil. Broil the eggplants on the center rack until the topping is golden brown, 2 to 4 minutes. Garnish with the basil.

Nutrition:

Calories: 360   Carbs: 35g   Sodium: 300mg

Fat: 22g   Protein: 14g   Potassium: 950mg

105.   Chicken Caesar Pasta Salad

Preparation time: 30 minutes   Cooking time: 20 minutes   Servings: 2

Ingredients:

- 4 oz. whole-wheat penne
- 1 1/2 cups shredded cooked chicken breast
- 1 cup cherry tomatoes, halved
- 3 cups chopped romaine lettuce
- 1/4 cup grated parmesan cheese
- 1/4 cup low-fat plain Greek yogurt
- 2 tbsp. fresh lemon juice

Directions:

1. Cook the pasta according to package directions, omitting salt. Drain and let it cool.
2. In a large bowl, combine the cooked pasta, chicken, tomatoes, and romaine lettuce.
3. In a small bowl, mix Greek yogurt, lemon juice, and parmesan cheese. Pour the dressing over the salad and mix well.
4. Serve immediately or refrigerate for up to 2 days.

Nutrition:

Calories: 455   Carbs: 50g   Sodium: 350mg

Fat: 12g   Protein: 38g   Potassium: 800mg

12.Snack

106.   Pumpkin Pie Fat Bombs

Preparation Time: 35 minutes   Cooking Time: 5 minutes   Servings: 2

Ingredients:

- 1 tbsp. coconut oil
- 2 1/2 tbsp. pumpkin puree
- 2 tbsp. almond butter
- 1 1/2 oz. sugar-free dark chocolate
- 3/4 tsp. pumpkin pie spice mix
- Stevia to taste

Directions:

1. Melt almond butter and dark chocolate over a double boiler. Divide the mixture between 4 small silicone molds or paper-lined mini muffin cups. Freeze until the crust has set.
2. In a small saucepan, combine the coconut oil, pumpkin puree, pumpkin pie spice, and stevia. Heat on low until softened and mix well. Pour over the chocolate layer.
3. Chill for 1 hour, then serve.

Nutrition:

Calories: 124   Protein: 3g   Sodium: 0mg

Carbs: 3g   Fat: 13g   Potassium: 142mg

107.   Sweet Almond and Coconut Fat Bombs

Preparation Time: 10 minutes   Cooking Time: 0 minutes   Servings: 2

Ingredients:

- 2 tbsp. melted coconut oil
- 4 1/2 tbsp. almond butter
- Liquid Stevia, to taste
- 1 1/2 tbsp. cocoa powder
- 3 tbsp. melted butter, salted

Directions:

1. In a bowl, mix all of the ingredients until well combined.
2. Pour the mixture into 4 small silicone molds or paper-lined mini muffin cups.
3. Chill for 20 minutes, remove from molds, and serve.

Nutrition:

Calories: 216   Protein: 5g   Sodium: 60mg

Carbohydrates: 4g   Fat: 21g   Potassium: 188mg

108.   Apricot Biscotti

Preparation Time: 10 minutes   Cooking Time: 50 minutes   Servings: 2

Ingredients:

- 1/4 cup whole wheat flour
- 1/4 cup all-purpose flour
- 2 tbsp. dark honey
- 1/4 cup chopped almonds
- 1/3 cup dried apricots, chopped
- 1 tbsp. milk, low-fat
- 1 egg, beaten lightly

Directions:

1. Preheat the oven to 350°F (175°C). Line a baking sheet with parchment paper.
2. In a bowl, mix the whole wheat flour, all-purpose flour, and honey. Add the beaten egg and milk, and mix until it forms a smooth dough. Fold in the chopped apricots and almonds.
3. Shape the dough into a small log (approximately 6 inches long and 1.5 inches wide) on the prepared baking sheet.
4. Bake for 25 minutes, or until the log turns golden brown. Remove from the oven and allow it to cool for 10 minutes.
5. Carefully slice the log into 1/2-inch thick slices. Lay the slices flat on the baking sheet and bake for an additional 10-15 minutes, or until the biscotti become crispy.
6. Remove from the oven, let cool, and serve.

Nutrition:

Calories: 445   Sodium: 75mg   Protein: 12g

Fat: 10g   Carbs: 82g   Potassium: 795mg

109. Apple and Berry Cobbler

Preparation Time: 10 minutes   Cooking Time: 40 minutes   Servings: 2

Ingredients:

Filling:

- 1 cup mixed blueberries and raspberries, fresh
- 1 cup apples, chopped
- 1 tbsp brown sugar
- 1/2 tsp ground cinnamon
- 1 tbsp cornstarch

Topping:

- 1/2 cup whole wheat pastry flour
- 1 tbsp brown sugar
- 1/8 cup soy milk or low-fat milk

Directions:

1. Preheat your oven to 350°F (175°C) and grease two small ramekins with cooking spray.
2. In a bowl, mix together the blueberries, raspberries, chopped apples, brown sugar, cinnamon, and cornstarch until the cornstarch dissolves.
3. In a separate bowl, whisk together the whole wheat pastry flour, brown sugar, and soy milk or low-fat milk until smooth.
4. Divide the berry mixture between the two ramekins and top each with the flour topping.
5. Place the ramekins on a baking sheet and bake for 30-40 minutes, or until the top is golden brown.
6. Remove from the oven, let cool slightly, and serve.

Nutrition:

Calories: 263   Sodium: 29mg   Protein: 6g

Fat: 1g   Carbs: 61g   Potassium: 310mg

110. Mixed Fruit Compote Cups

Preparation Time: 5 minutes   Cooking Time: 15 minutes   Servings: 2

Ingredients:

- 1 1/4 cup water
- 1/2 cup orange juice
- 12 ounces mixed dried fruit
- 1 teaspoon ground cinnamon
- 1/4 teaspoon ground ginger
- 1/4 teaspoon ground nutmeg
- 4 cups vanilla frozen yogurt, fat-free

Directions:

1. Mix your dried fruit, nutmeg, cinnamon, water, orange juice, and ginger in a saucepan.
2. Cover, and allow it to cook over medium heat for ten minutes. Remove the cover and then cook for another ten minutes.
3. Add your frozen yogurt to serving cups, and top with the fruit mixture.

Nutrition:

Calories: 228   Sodium: 114mg   Protein: 9.1g

Fat: 5.7g   Carbs: 2.4g   Potassium: 143.8mg

111. Generous Garlic Bread Stick

Preparation time: 15 minutes   Cooking time: 15 minutes   Servings: 2

Ingredients:

- 1/4 cup almond flour
- 1/8 teaspoon garlic powder
- 1/4 teaspoon baking powder
- 1/2 tablespoon psyllium husk powder
- 1 tablespoon almond butter, softened
- 1/2 egg
- 2 tablespoons boiling water

Directions:

1. Preheat your oven to 400°F (200°C).
2. Line a baking sheet with parchment paper and set aside.
3. In a bowl, mix almond flour, garlic powder, baking powder, and psyllium husk powder.
4. Add softened almond butter and the half egg, mixing well.

5. Pour boiling water into the mix and stir until you have a nice dough.
6. Divide the dough into 2 balls and roll into breadsticks.
7. Place on the baking sheet and bake for 15 minutes.
8. Remove from the oven, let cool slightly, and enjoy!

Nutrition:

Calories: 159	Protein: 7g	Sodium: 24mg
Carbs: 7g	Fat: 24g	Potassium: 182mg

112. Cauliflower Bread Stick

Preparation time: 10 minutes   Cooking time: 48 minutes   Servings: 2

Ingredients:

- 1/2 cup cauliflower rice, cooked for 3 minutes in microwave
- 1/2 tablespoon almond butter
- 1/2 egg
- 1/4 teaspoon Italian seasoning
- 1/8 teaspoon red pepper flakes
- 1/4 cup low-fat cheese (mozzarella or ricotta)
- 1 teaspoon garlic, minced

Directions:

1. Preheat your oven to 350°F (175°C).
2. In a small pan, melt almond butter over low heat. Add red pepper flakes and garlic, cooking for 2-3 minutes.
3. Add the garlic and almond butter mix to the bowl with cooked cauliflower. Add Italian seasoning.
4. Mix well and refrigerate for 10 minutes.
5. Add cheese and the half egg to the bowl and mix.
6. Place a layer of parchment paper at the bottom of a small baking dish and grease with cooking spray. Add the cauliflower mixture.
7. Bake for 30 minutes, remove from oven and sprinkle with a bit of additional cheese, if desired.
8. Bake for another 8 minutes. Remove from oven, let cool slightly, and enjoy!

Nutrition:

Calories: 149	Protein: 10.7g	Sodium: 5mg
Carbs: 11.5g	Fat: 20g	Potassium: 192.6mg

113. Cocktail Wieners

Preparation time: 2 minutes   Cooking Time: 1 minutes   Servings: 2

Ingredients:

- 4 cocktail wieners
- 1/8 teaspoon brown sugar
- 1/4 cup chicken or veggie broth
- 1 tablespoon jalapeño jelly
- 1 tablespoon chili sauce
- 1/2 diced jalapeño

Directions:

1. Place 1/4 cup of chicken broth into an instant pot, then add wieners and the rest of the ingredients, stirring until everything is coated.
2. Cook on high pressure for 1 minute, quick release pressure, then serve.

Nutrition:

Calories: 92	Carbs: 6g	Sodium: 4mg
Fat: 5g	Protein: 10g	Potassium: 176.3

114. Pressure Cooker Braised Pulled Ham

Preparation time: 10 minutes   Cooking Time: 25 minutes   Servings: 2

Ingredients:

- 1/2 cup beer or non-alcoholic beer
- 1/8 teaspoon coarse ground pepper
- 1/4 cup Dijon mustard, divided
- 8 oz cooked bone-in ham
- 1 small rosemary sprig

Directions:

1. Whisk the beer, pepper, and mustard, and then add ham and rosemary to the pressure cooker.
2. Lock the lid and set pressure to high for 20 minutes, then allow for a natural pressure release.

3. Let the ham cool, discard rosemary, and shred the ham with forks, discarding the bone.
4. Serve the shredded ham on whole wheat bread or whole grain crackers, adding Dijon mustard as desired.

Nutrition:

Calories: 378	Carbs: 5g	Sodium: 7mg
Fat: 9g	Protein: 25g	Potassium: 179mg

115. Mini Teriyaki Turkey Sandwiches

Preparation time: 20 minutes   Cooking Time: 30 minutes   Servings: 2

Ingredients:

- 1 small chicken breast
- 1/4 cup low-sodium soy sauce
- 1 tablespoon cider vinegar
- 1 small garlic clove, minced
- 1/4 teaspoon fresh ginger root, minced
- 1/2 tablespoon cornstarch
- 2 whole wheat rolls

Directions:

1. Place the chicken in a pressure cooker and combine the soy sauce, vinegar, garlic, and ginger over it.
2. Cook on manual for 25 minutes, and when finished, allow for a natural pressure release.
3. Remove the chicken and set the cooker to sauté. Mix cornstarch with a little water, stir into the cooking juices, and cook until the sauce thickens. Shred the chicken and stir to heat.
4. Split the whole wheat rolls and serve the shredded chicken on top.

Nutrition:

Calories: 252	Carbs: 5g	Sodium: 42mg
Fat: 5g	Protein: 26g	Potassium: 186.3mg

116. Peach Crumble Muffins

Preparation Time: 25 minutes   Cooking Time: 25 minutes   Servings: 2

Ingredients:

For the crumble:

- 1 teaspoon dark brown sugar
- 1/2 teaspoon ground cinnamon
- 1 teaspoon canola oil
- 2 tablespoons old-fashioned rolled oats

For the peach muffins:

- 1/4 teaspoon baking powder
- 1/4 teaspoon baking soda
- 1/8 teaspoon salt
- 1 tablespoon canola oil
- 1 tablespoon dark brown sugar
- 1/2 large egg
- 1/2 peach, diced
- 1/2 cup whole wheat flour or whole wheat pastry flour

Directions:

1. In a small bowl, mix the brown sugar, cinnamon, canola oil, and oats for the crumble. For the muffins, mix the flour, baking powder, baking soda, and salt in a large bowl.
2. In a separate bowl, beat the canola oil, brown sugar, and the half egg using a hand mixer until fluffy.
3. Add the flour mixture to the wet ingredients and mix until just combined.
4. Fold in the diced peach with a spatula. Preheat the oven to 425°F. Grease a muffin tin for 2 muffins.
5. Fill each muffin cup with batter about three-quarters of the way full. Scoop the crumble mixture on top of each.
6. Bake for 5 to 6 minutes, then reduce the oven temperature to 350°F and bake for 15 to 18 additional minutes. Cool before removing from the muffin tin. Once completely cooled, serve.

Nutrition:

Calories: 310	Carbs: 40g	Sodium: 200mg
Fat: 14g	Protein: 8g	Potassium: 190mg

117. Cranberry Hot Wings

Preparation time: 45 minutes   Cooking Time: 35 minutes   Servings: 2 dozen

Ingredients:

- 1/2 can jellied cranberry sauce (low-sodium)
- 2 tablespoons Louisiana-style hot sauce

- 1 tablespoon honey
- 1 tablespoon Dijon mustard (low-sodium)
- 1/4 cup sugar-free orange juice
- 1 pound chicken wings
- 1 teaspoon cornstarch

Directions:
1. In a bowl, whisk together cranberry sauce, hot sauce, honey, Dijon mustard, and orange juice. Set aside.
2. Trim chicken wings and discard wing tips.
3. Place chicken wings in your Instant Pot and pour the cranberry mixture over them.
4. Lock the lid and set pressure to high for 10 minutes.
5. Allow for natural pressure release, then carefully release any remaining pressure.
6. Preheat broiler. Transfer wings to a foil-lined baking sheet and broil for 10-12 minutes, turning once, until browned.
7. Meanwhile, heat the remaining cranberry mixture in a saucepan over medium heat. Mix 1 teaspoon of cornstarch with 1 tablespoon of cold water, then stir it into the sauce to thicken slightly.
8. Brush the cooked wings with the thickened glaze before serving.

Nutrition:

Calories: 355

Fat: 20g

Carbs: 25g

Protein: 20g

Sodium: 210mg

Potassium: 295mg

118.   Almond and Tomato Balls

Preparation Time: 10 minutes   Cooking Time: 0 minutes   Servings: 2

Ingredients:

- 1/6 cup almonds, chopped
- 5 ounces low-fat cream cheese
- 1/6 cup sun-dried tomatoes, diced

Directions:
1. Chop almonds into small pieces.
2. In a bowl, combine cream cheese and sun-dried tomatoes. Mix well.
3. Chill the mixture for 15-20 minutes and then form into balls.
4. Roll the balls in the chopped almonds.
5. Serve and enjoy!

Nutrition:

Calories: 186

Fat: 13g

Carbs: 8g

Protein: 11g

Sodium: 150mg

Potassium: 310mg

119.   Avocado Tuna Bites

Preparation Time: 10 minutes   Cooking Time: 0 minutes   Servings: 2

Ingredients:

- 1/6 cup coconut oil
- 1/2 avocado, cut into cubes
- 5 ounces canned tuna, drained (low-sodium)
- 1/8 cup Parmesan cheese, grated
- 1/8 teaspoon garlic powder
- 1/8 teaspoon onion powder
- 1/6 cup almond flour

Directions:
1. In a bowl, mix tuna, almond flour, Parmesan cheese, garlic powder, and onion powder.
2. Gently fold in avocado cubes.
3. Form 6 balls from the mixture.
4. Heat coconut oil in a pan over medium heat and cook the balls until golden on all sides.
5. Serve and enjoy!

Nutrition:

Calories: 254

Fat: 20g

Carbs: 4g

Protein: 17g

Sodium: 160mg

Potassium: 375mg

120. Hearty Buttery Walnuts

Preparation Time: 10 minutes   Cooking Time: 0 minutes   Servings: 2

Ingredients:

- 2 walnut halves
- 1/2 tablespoon almond butter

Directions:

1. Spread almond butter over one walnut half.
2. Top with the other walnut half.
3. Serve and enjoy!

Nutrition:

Calories: 95	Carbs: 2g	Sodium: 0.5mg
Fat: 9g	Protein: 2g	Potassium: 64.7mg

121. Refreshing Watermelon Sorbet

Preparation Time: 10 minutes + 4-6 hours chill time   Cooking Time: 0 minutes   Servings: 4

Ingredients:

- 2 cups watermelon, seedless and chunked
- 2 tablespoons of coconut sugar
- 1 tablespoon lime juice

Directions:

1. Add the ingredients to a blender and puree. Freeze the mixture for about 4-6 hours until you have a gelatin-like consistency.
2. Puree the mixture once again and return to the container. Chill overnight. Allow the sorbet to stand for 5 minutes before serving.

Nutrition:

Calories: 91	Carbs: 23g	Sodium: 0mg
Fat: 0g	Protein: 1g	Potassium: 138mg

122. Faux Mac and Cheese

Preparation Time: 15 minutes   Cooking Time: 30-45 minutes   Servings: 2

Ingredients:

- 2 1/2 cups cauliflower florets
- Salt and pepper to taste
- 1/2 cup of coconut milk
- 1/4 cup vegetable broth
- 1 tablespoon coconut flour, sifted
- 1 cup cheddar cheese

Directions:

1. Preheat your oven to 350F. Season florets with salt and steam until firm. Place florets in a greased ovenproof dish. Heat up coconut milk over medium heat in a skillet; season with salt and pepper.
2. Stir in broth and add coconut flour to the mix, stir. Cook until the sauce begins to bubble. Remove from heat. Pour the thick sauce over cauliflower and mix in cheese. Bake for 30-45 minutes.

Nutrition:

Calories: 229	Carbs: 9g	Sodium: 25mg
Fat: 14g	Protein: 15g	Potassium: 158.2mg

123. Banana Custard

Preparation Time: 10 minutes   Cooking Time: 25 minutes   Servings: 2

Ingredients:

- 1 ripe banana, peeled and mashed finely
- 1/4 teaspoon of vanilla extract
- 7 ounces unsweetened almond milk
- 2 eggs

Directions:

1. Preheat your oven to 350F. Grease 4 custard glasses lightly. Arrange the glasses in a large baking dish. In a large bowl, mix all of the ingredients until combined nicely.
2. Divide the mixture evenly between the glasses. Pour water into the baking dish. Bake for 25 minutes. Remove from oven and serve.

Nutrition:

Calories: 177	Carbs: 17g	Sodium: 92mg
Fat: 8.8g	Protein: 9g	Potassium: 254mg

124. Healthy Tahini Buns

Preparation Time: 10 minutes	Cooking Time: 15-20 minutes	Servings: 2

Ingredients:

- 1 whole egg
- 2 1/2 tablespoons tahini paste
- 1/4 teaspoon baking soda
- 1/2 teaspoon lemon juice
- A pinch of salt

Directions:

1. Preheat your oven to 350F. Line a baking sheet with parchment paper and set aside. Combine the ingredients in a bowl and mix until you have a smooth batter.
2. Scoop the batter onto the prepared sheet, forming buns. Bake for 15-20 minutes. Remove from the oven and let them cool before serving.

Nutrition:

Calories: 172	Protein: 6g	Sodium: 12mg
Carbs: 7g	Fat: 14g	Potassium: 132mg

125. Sautéed Swiss Chard

Preparation time: 5 minutes	Cooking time: 10 minutes	Servings: 2

Ingredients:

- 7.5 oz Swiss chard, chopped
- 1/4 cup of soy milk
- 1/2 teaspoon chili powder
- 1/2 tablespoon avocado oil
- 1/2 teaspoon whole-grain wheat flour
- 1/8 onion, diced

Directions:

1. Warm the avocado oil in a pan and add the diced onion. Sauté for 3 minutes.
2. Stir well and add flour and soy milk. Whisk the mixture until smooth.
3. Add the chopped Swiss chard and gently mix the ingredients.
4. Cover the pan and sauté the side dish for 5 minutes over medium-low heat.

Nutrition:

Calories: 80	Carbs: 10g	Sodium: 150mg
Fat: 2g	Protein: 6g	Potassium: 220mg

126. Asian Style Asparagus

Preparation time: 5 minutes	Cooking time: 10 minutes	Servings: 2

Ingredients:

- 8 oz. asparagus, chopped
- 1 tablespoon balsamic vinegar
- 1 teaspoon lime zest, grated
- 1 teaspoon sesame seeds
- 1/4 teaspoon ground cumin
- 2 tablespoons avocado oil or canola oil

Directions:

1. Heat 1 tablespoon of avocado oil or canola oil in a skillet and add the chopped asparagus.
2. Add the lime zest and sauté the vegetables for 5 minutes, stirring occasionally.
3. Sprinkle the vegetables with ground cumin and add the remaining oil.
4. Roast the asparagus for 5 minutes at 400F in the oven.
5. After cooking, drizzle the vegetables with balsamic vinegar and sesame seeds. Toss the side dish well to combine.

Nutrition:

Calories: 130	Carbs: 5 g	Sodium: 30 mg
Fat: 11 g	Protein: 3 g	Potassium: 150 mg

127.   Aromatic Cauliflower Florets

Preparation time: 7 minutes   Cooking time: 18 minutes   Servings: 2

Ingredients:

- 1/2-pound cauliflower florets
- 1/2 tablespoon curry powder
- 2 tablespoons of soy milk
- 1/2 tablespoon avocado oil or canola oil
- 1/4 teaspoon dried oregano

Directions:

1. Preheat the oven to 375F.
2. Heat the avocado oil or canola oil in a saucepan.
3. Combine soy milk and curry powder and whisk the liquid until smooth.
4. Pour it into the saucepan with the oil and bring to a boil.
5. Add cauliflower florets and stir well.
6. Then, close the lid and cook the vegetables for 5 minutes. Transfer the pan to the preheated oven and cook the meal for 10 minutes, until the florets are soft.

Nutrition:

Calories 80   Carbs 10 g   Sodium 60 mg
Fat 4 g   Protein 2 g   Potassium 270 mg

128.   Brussel Sprouts Mix

Preparation time: 6 minutes   Cooking time: 15 minutes   Servings: 2

Ingredients:

- 1 cup Brussel sprouts, sliced
- 1 tablespoon olive oil
- 1 tomato, chopped
- 1/2 cup fresh parsley, chopped
- 2 oz. leek, sliced
- 1 cup low-sodium vegetable broth
- 1/2 jalapeno pepper, chopped

Directions:

1. Pour the olive oil into a saucepan.
2. Add the sliced Brussels sprouts and leek and cook for 5 minutes. Stir the vegetables occasionally.
3. Add the parsley, chopped tomato, jalapeno, and low-sodium vegetable broth.
4. Close the lid and cook at medium-high heat for 10 min. Stir the vegetables during cooking to avoid burning them.

Nutrition:

Calories: 65   Carbs: 15 g   Sodium: 80 mg
Fat: 4 g   Protein: 3 g   Potassium: 140 mg

129.   Braised Baby Carrot

Preparation time: 5 minutes   Cooking time: 22 minutes   Servings: 2

Ingredients:

- 1 cup baby carrots
- 1 teaspoon dried thyme
- 1 tablespoon olive oil
- 1/2 cup low-sodium vegetable stock
- 1 garlic clove, sliced

Directions:

1. Heat the olive oil in the saucepan for 30 seconds.
2. Then add the sliced garlic and dried thyme. Set the mixture to a boil and add the baby carrot.
3. Roast the vegetables for 7 min over medium heat. Stir them constantly.
4. Then, add low-sodium vegetable stock and close the lid.
5. Cook the baby carrots for 15 min until they are tender.

Nutrition:

Calories: 69   Carbs: 1 g   Sodium: 10 mg
Fat: 5 g   Protein: 2 g   Potassium: 140 mg

130.   Acorn Squash with Apples

Preparation time: 20-25 minutes   Cooking time: 5-7 minutes   Servings: 2

Ingredients:

- 1 Granny Smith apple
- 2 tablespoons brown sugar

- 1 Acorn squash, small or about 6 inches in diameter
- 2 teaspoons margarine - trans-fat-free

Directions:

1. Peel the apple, then remove the core and slice.
2. Toss the apple and brown sugar. Set aside.
3. Poke a few holes in the squash. Place it into the microwave for 5 min using the high-power setting.
4. Turn the squash over after three minutes.
5. Put it on the chopping block and slice it in half. Discard the seeds and load the hollowed squash with the apple mixture.
6. Set the container back in the microwave and continue cooking the apples until they're softened (2 min.).
7. Serve the squash with a portion of margarine.

Nutrition:

Calories: 209   Carbs: 3.2 g   Sodium: 25 mg

Fat: 4 g   Protein: 3 g   Potassium: 50 mg

131.   Asparagus with Horseradish Dip

Preparation time: 15 minutes   Cooking time: 5 minutes   Servings: 2

Ingredients:

- 4 fresh asparagus spears
- 1/4 cup reduced-fat mayonnaise
- 1 tablespoon grated parmesan cheese

- 1/2 teaspoon prepared horseradish
- 1/8 teaspoon Worcestershire sauce

Directions:

1. Trim and place the asparagus in a steamer basket in a large saucepan (over one inch of water).
2. Wait for it to boil by covering. Steam until crisp-tender (2-4 min.).
3. Drain and immediately place it into ice water to chill. Drain it into a colander and pat dry.
4. Combine the rest of the dressings.
5. Serve with the asparagus.

Nutrition:

Calories: 110   Carbs: 3 g   Sodium: 225 mg

Fat: 9.5 g   Protein: 2 g   Potassium: 108 mg

132.   Grilled Tomatoes

Preparation time: 10 minutes   Cooking time: 2 minutes   Servings: 2

Ingredients:

- 2 tomatoes
- 1/4 teaspoon dried basil

- 1/2 tablespoon olive oil
- 1/4 teaspoon dried oregano

Directions:

1. Preheat the grill to 390F.
2. Slice the tomatoes and sprinkle with dried oregano and dried basil.
3. Then, drizzle the vegetables with olive oil and place them in the preheated grill.
4. Grill the tomatoes for 1 minute on each side.
5. Use a metal scoop to lift the tomatoes off the grill. Serve.

Nutrition:

Calories: 60   Carbs: 6 g   Sodium: 10 mg

Fat: 3.5 g   Protein: 1 g   Potassium: 364 mg

133.   Parsley Celery Root

Preparation time: 7 minutes   Cooking time: 20 minutes   Servings: 2

Ingredients:

- 1 cup celery root, chopped
- 1 oz. fresh parsley, chopped
- 1/2 tablespoon margarine
- 1/2 teaspoon olive oil
- 1/2 teaspoon cumin seeds
- 1/8 cup of water

Directions:
1. Mix up olive oil and margarine in the skillet.
2. Add cumin seeds and heat the mixture for 1-2 minutes or until you get the light cumin smell.
3. Then, add chopped celery root and roast it for 8 minutes (for 4 minutes from each side).
4. Then add water and parsley. Close the lid.
5. Cook the vegetables for 8 minutes on medium-low heat or until it is tender.

Nutrition:

Calories: 120	Carbs: 11 g	Sodium: 60 mg
Fat: 8 g	Protein: 2 g	Potassium: 395 mg

134.   Garlic Black Eyed Peas

Preparation Time: 5 minutes   Cooking Time: 120 minutes   Servings: 2

Ingredients:

- 1 garlic clove, diced
- 3 tbsp black-eyed peas, soaked
- 1/2 tbsp shallot, chopped
- 1/2 tbsp avocado oil
- 1/2 tsp cayenne pepper
- 1 cup water

Directions:
1. In a skillet, mix garlic, shallot, cayenne pepper, and avocado oil.
2. Sauté the mixture for 1 minute.
3. Add black-eyed peas and water.
4. Close the lid and cook the meal over low heat for 2 hours or until the black-eyed peas are soft.

Nutrition:

Calories: 100	Carbs: 12 g	Sodium: 8 mg
Fat: 4 g	Protein: 3 g	Potassium: 211 mg

135.   Braised Artichokes

Preparation time: 10 minutes   Cooking time: 35 minutes   Servings: 2

Ingredients:

- 2 artichokes, trimmed
- 2 garlic cloves, minced
- 2 tbsp olive oil
- 1/2 lemon
- 1/2 cup water
- 1/2 tsp dried cilantro

Directions:
1. Squeeze the juice from the lemon into a saucepan.
2. Add water.
3. In a shallow bowl, mix garlic, olive oil, and dried cilantro.
4. Rub the artichokes with the garlic mixture and place them in the lemon and water.
5. Close the lid and cook vegetables for 35 minutes or until tender.
6. Drizzle the cooked artichokes with the lemon and water mixture. Serve.

Nutrition:

Calories: 172	Carbs: 12 g	Sodium: 52 mg
Fat: 14 g	Protein: 3 g	Potassium: 249 mg

136.   Grilled Eggplant Slices

Preparation time: 5 minutes   Cooking time: 15-20 minutes   Servings: 2

Ingredients:

- 1 eggplant
- 1/2 garlic clove
- 1/8 tsp dried dill
- 2 1/2 tbsp extra virgin olive oil
- 1/8 tsp salt
- black pepper

Directions:

1. Wash the eggplant and dry it well. Divide it into slices about half an inch thick.
2. Heat a grill pan and place the eggplant slices in it, a few at a time.
3. Let them grill for a few minutes, first on one side and then on the other. Set them on a plate as they are ready.
4. Prepare the marinade: pour the oil into a small bowl, add a pinch of salt and ground pepper, and the chopped garlic clove. Stir everything with a fork until the salt is completely dissolved.
5. Brush the eggplants with the marinade and arrange them in layers on a serving plate. Let the grilled eggplant rest before serving.

Nutrition:

Calories: 127	Carbs: 4 g	Sodium: 163 mg
Fat: 14 g	Protein: 1 g	Potassium: 235 mg

137.   Lentil Sauté

Preparation time: 5 minutes Cooking time: 40 minutes Servings: 4

Ingredients:

- 1/4 cup lentils
- 1/2 cup spinach
- 2 cups of water
- 1/2 teaspoon cayenne pepper
- 1/4 teaspoon ground coriander
- 1/2 garlic clove, minced
- 1/2 tomato, chopped

Directions:

1. Mix all ingredients in a saucepan and stir them gently.
2. Cover and cook the sauté for 40 minutes on medium-high heat.

Nutrition:

Calories: 115	Carbs: 20 g	Sodium: 8 mg
Fat: 1 g	Protein: 8 g	Potassium: 364 mg

138.   Italian Style Zucchini Coins

Preparation time: 10 minutes Cooking time: 5 minutes Servings: 2

Ingredients:

- 2 zucchinis, sliced
- 1/2 tablespoon Italian seasonings
- 1 tablespoon avocado oil
- 1/8 teaspoon garlic powder

Directions:

1. In a small bowl, mix Italian seasonings and garlic powder.
2. Coat the zucchini slices with the seasoning mixture.
3. Heat the avocado oil in a skillet over medium heat.
4. Place the zucchini slices in the pan in a single layer and cook for 1 min on each side or until lightly browned.
5. Transfer the zucchini to a plate lined with a paper towel to absorb excess oil.

Nutrition:

Calories: 99	Carbs: 8 g	Sodium: 6 mg
Fat: 7 g	Protein: 3 g	Potassium: 573 mg

139.   Brussels sprouts with Shallots and Lemon

Preparation time: 25 minutes Cooking time: 10 minutes Servings: 2

Ingredients:

- 1 1/2 teaspoon avocado oil, divided
- 1 1/2 tablespoon shallots, sliced thin
- 1/8 teaspoon salt, divided
- 1/2 lb. Brussels sprouts
- 1/4 cup low-sodium vegetable stock
- 1/8 teaspoon finely grated lemon zest
- 1/2 tablespoon fresh squeezed lemon juice
- 1/8 teaspoon black pepper

Directions:

1. Heat a large, nonstick skillet over medium heat and add 1 teaspoon of avocado oil. Sauté the shallots until softened and lightly golden (about 6 minutes).
2. Stir in 1/8 teaspoon salt. Transfer to a bowl and set aside.

3. In the same pan, heat the remaining 1/2 teaspoon of avocado oil over medium heat.
4. Cut the Brussels sprouts into quarters and add them to the pan, sautéing for 3-4 minutes.
5. Add the low-sodium vegetable stock and simmer, covered, until the Brussels sprouts are tender (about 5-6 minutes).
6. Stir in the cooked shallots, lemon zest, lemon juice, black pepper, and remaining 1/8 teaspoon salt.
7. Serve immediately.

Nutrition:

Calories: 135	Carbs: 18 g	Sodium: 204 mg
Fat: 5 g	Protein: 5 g	Potassium: 586 mg

140.   Chili-Lime Grilled Pineapple

Preparation Time: 15 minutes   Cooking time: 2-6 minutes   Servings: 2

Ingredients:

- 1 fresh pineapple
- 1/2 tablespoon honey or agave nectar
- 1 1/2 tablespoon brown sugar
- 1/2 tablespoon lime juice

- 1/2 tablespoon avocado oil
- 1/8 teaspoon salt
- 3/4 teaspoon chili powder

Directions:

1. Peel pineapple, removing any eyes from the fruit. Cut lengthwise into three wedges; remove the core.
2. In a small bowl, mix honey, brown sugar, lime juice, avocado oil, salt, and chili powder.
3. Coat the pineapple wedges with half of the glaze; reserve the remaining mixture for basting.
4. Grill the pineapple on medium heat, covered, until lightly browned (2-4 minutes per side), basting occasionally with the reserved glaze.

Nutrition:

Calories: 218	Carbs: 46 g	Sodium: 150 mg
Fat: 4 g	Protein: 1 g	Potassium: 227 mg

13. Veggies

141.   Zucchini Fritters with Corn Salsa

Preparation Time: 10 minutes   Cooking time: 10 minutes   Servings: 2

Ingredients:

For the salsa:

- 1 cup cherry tomatoes, diced, juices reserved
- 1/2 cup corn kernels (thawed, if frozen)
- 1/4 cup chopped fresh cilantro
- 1/2 tablespoon freshly squeezed lime juice
- 1/2 tablespoon avocado oil

For the fritters

- 1 large zucchini, grated, about 2 cups
- 1/2 of 15-ounce can low-sodium cannellini beans, rinsed and drained
- 1 large egg white
- 1 1/2 tablespoons chopped fresh parsley
- 1 garlic clove, minced
- 1/8 teaspoon sea salt
- 1/4 cup almond flour

Directions:

1. To make the salsa, combine tomatoes, corn, cilantro, lime juice, and avocado oil in a medium bowl. Season with black pepper to taste. Set aside for 30 minutes to let flavors meld.
2. Preheat the air fryer to 370F.
3. Pat the grated zucchini dry using a dish towel or paper towel to remove any excess water.
4. In a bowl, combine zucchini, beans, egg white, parsley, garlic, salt, and almond flour. Slightly mash the beans while mixing. Using damp hands, form the zucchini mixture into 8 patties.
5. Cook the patties in a single layer in the air fryer basket for 12 minutes, until golden brown. Serve the fritters topped with salsa.

Nutrition:

Calories: 228   Sodium: 114 mg   Protein: 9.1 g

Fat: 5.7 g   Carbs: 30 g   Potassium: 480 mg

142.   Zucchini Lasagna Roll-Ups

Preparation Time: 20 minutes   Cooking time: 10 minutes   Servings: 2

Ingredients:

- 1 cup part-skim ricotta cheese
- 1/4 cup low-sodium cannellini beans, drained, rinsed, and mashed
- 1 large zucchini, cut lengthwise into ⅛-inch-thick strips
- 1/2 tablespoon granulated garlic
- 1/2 tablespoon dried basil
- 1/2 tablespoon dried oregano
- 1 cup low-sodium marinara sauce

Directions:

1. Preheat the air fryer to 400F.
2. In a medium bowl, combine ricotta cheese, mashed beans, granulated garlic, dried basil, and dried oregano.
3. Lay the zucchini slices flat in a single layer. Spread 1 tablespoon of the ricotta mixture along each zucchini slice. Roll up each slice and secure with a toothpick.
4. Place the zucchini roll-ups in the air fryer basket in a single layer and cook for 10 minutes.
5. While the zucchini roll-ups are cooking, heat the marinara sauce on the stovetop over medium heat until warm. Serve the zucchini roll-ups topped with marinara sauce.

Nutrition:

Calories: 205   Carbs: 20 g   Sodium: 16.2 mg

Fat: 1 g   Protein: 9 g   Potassium: 197.4 mg

143.   Toasted Chickpea-Quinoa Bowl

Preparation Time: 20 minutes   Cooking time: 10 minutes   Servings: 2

Ingredients:

- 1/2 (15-ounce) can low-sodium chickpeas, drained and rinsed
- 1 large zucchini, chopped
- 1 1/2 cups coarsely chopped cauliflower florets
- 1/2 tablespoon extra-virgin olive oil
- 1/2 teaspoon paprika
- 1/4 cup dry quinoa
- 2 cups fresh arugula

Directions:

1. In a bowl, mix the chickpeas, zucchini, cauliflower, olive oil, and paprika.
2. Place the chickpea and vegetable mixture in the air fryer basket in a single layer. Set the temperature to 350F and cook for 4 minutes. Shake or stir and cook for 4 more minutes, until the vegetables are tender.
3. Cook the quinoa according to the package directions.
4. To assemble, divide the quinoa and arugula between bowls, top with the chickpeas and vegetables.

Nutrition:

Calories: 295	Carbs: 43 g	Sodium: 15 mg
Fat: 9 g	Protein: 15 g	Potassium: 121 mg

144.   Fried Pasta Chips

Preparation Time: 20 minutes   Cooking time: 15 minutes   Servings: 2

Ingredients:

- 6 ounces chickpea pasta
- 1 tablespoon extra-virgin olive oil
- 2 tablespoons nutritional yeast
- 1/2 teaspoon dried basil
- 1/2 teaspoon dried oregano
- 1/2 teaspoon granulated garlic
- 1/8 teaspoon sea salt

Directions:

1. Preheat the air fryer to 375°F.
2. Cook the pasta in boiling water until al dente, about 8 minutes.
3. Transfer the pasta to a large bowl and drizzle with the olive oil. Stir in the nutritional yeast, basil, oregano, garlic, and salt.
4. Place the pasta in the air fryer basket in a single layer and cook for 5 minutes. Shake or stir, then continue to cook for another 2 to 3 minutes, until the pasta is golden brown.
5. Transfer to a paper-towel–lined plate and allow to cool before serving.

Nutrition:

Calories: 499	Fat: 20g	Sodium: 30mg
Carbs: 57g	Protein: 23g	Potassium: 107 mg

145.   Penne with Sizzling Tomatoes and Artichokes

Preparation Time: 20 minutes   Cooking time: 10 minutes   Servings: 2

Ingredients:

- 6 ounces chickpea penne
- 2 cups cherry tomatoes
- 1/2 (7-ounce) jar marinated artichoke hearts, drained and chopped
- 1 tablespoon extra-virgin olive oil
- 1/2 tablespoon dried basil
- 1/2 tablespoon dried oregano
- 1 teaspoon granulated garlic

Directions:

1. Preheat the air fryer to 375F. Cook the pasta according to package directions.
2. In a large bowl, mix the tomatoes, artichoke hearts, olive oil, basil, oregano, and garlic.
3. Line the air fryer basket with parchment paper or use an air fryer baking pan. Place the tomatoes and artichokes in the prepared basket and cook for 10 minutes.
4. Toss the cooked tomatoes and artichokes with the pasta and serve immediately.

Nutrition:

Calories: 374	Carbs: 48 g	Sodium: 26 mg
Fat: 12 g	Protein: 18 g	Potassium: 182.7 mg

146.   Black Bean Bake with Avocado

Preparation Time: 10 minutes   Cooking time: 10 minutes   Servings: 2

Ingredients:

- 1/2 (15-ounce) can low-sodium black beans, rinsed and drained
- 1 cup corn kernels (thawed, if frozen)
- 1 large bell pepper, diced
- 1 tablespoon extra-virgin olive oil
- 1 teaspoon ground cumin
- 3 tablespoons nutritional yeast
- 1/2 Hass avocado, sliced

Directions:

1. Preheat the air fryer to 375F.
2. In a bowl, mix the black beans, corn, bell pepper, olive oil, and cumin.
3. Spread the bean mixture in an air fryer baking pan and place it in the air fryer basket. Cook for 6 minutes.
4. Sprinkle the mixture with nutritional yeast and cook for another 3 minutes until the top is golden brown.
5. To serve, remove from the pan and top with the avocado slices.

Nutrition:

Calories: 315   Fat: 11 g   Sodium: 14 mg
Carbs: 43 g   Protein: 17 g   Potassium: 121.6 mg

147.   Falafel with Mint-Tahini Sauce

Preparation Time: 15 minutes   Cooking time: 10 minutes   Servings: 2

Ingredients:

For the falafel

- 1/2 cup dried chickpeas, soaked overnight, drained, rinsed, and patted dry
- 1/4 red onion, chopped
- 1/4 red bell pepper, chopped
- 1/4 cup fresh parsley, stemmed
- 1/2 teaspoon ground cumin
- 1 garlic clove, minced
- 1/2 teaspoon extra-virgin olive oil

For the mint-tahini sauce

- 1/4 cup tahini
- 1/4 cup chopped fresh mint
- 1 tablespoon freshly squeezed lemon juice

Directions:

To make the falafel

1. Preheat the air fryer to 350F.
2. In a food processor, combine the chickpeas, onion, bell pepper, parsley, cumin, and garlic. Pulse until well combined into a rough paste.
3. With damp hands, divide the falafel mixture into 5 patties, about 1 inch thick.
4. Lightly brush the patties with olive oil.
5. Working in batches if necessary, place the patties in a single layer in the air fryer basket. Set the temperature to 350F and cook for 8 minutes, flipping halfway through, or until golden brown.

To make the mint-tahini sauce

1. In a small bowl, stir together the tahini, mint, and lemon juice until smooth. If the sauce is too thick, add water, 1 tablespoon at a time, until it reaches a consistency thin enough for dipping.
2. Serve the warm falafel with the mint-tahini sauce.

Nutrition:

Calories: 403   Carbs: 42 g   Sodium: 34 mg
Fat: 23 g   Protein: 16 g   Potassium: 116 mg

148.   Quinoa-Lentil Burgers

Preparation Time: 20 minutes   Cooking time: 10 minutes   Servings: 2

Ingredients:

- 1/6 cup dry quinoa
- 1/2 cup dried red lentils
- 2 cups water
- 2 cups spinach
- 1/4 large red onion, chopped
- 1/4 cup almond flour

Directions:

1. In a saucepan, combine the quinoa, lentils, and water. Bring to a boil, then reduce heat, cover, and simmer for 15 minutes. In the last minute, add spinach and let wilt.
2. Drain the quinoa mixture and transfer to a large bowl. Stir in the red onion and almond flour. Cover and refrigerate for at least 30 minutes.
3. Preheat the air fryer to 350F.
4. Divide the burger mixture into 2 large patties, about 5 inches in diameter.
5. Place the burgers in a single layer in the air fryer basket and cook for 10 minutes. Flip the burgers over and cook for another 2 minutes, or until golden brown. Serve immediately over salad or in a whole wheat bun.

Nutrition:

Calories: 328	Carbs: 42g	Sodium: 20mg
Fat: 9g	Protein: 18g	Potassium: 128mg

149. Eggplant Bites with Marinara

Preparation Time: 20 minutes   Cooking time: 10 minutes   Servings: 2

Ingredients:

For the marinara sauce

- 1/2 tablespoon extra-virgin olive oil
- 1 garlic clove, minced
- 1 cup crushed tomatoes

For the eggplant bites

- 1/2 medium eggplant, skinned and cut into cubes
- 1/2 cup whole wheat panko bread crumbs
- 1 tablespoon extra-virgin olive oil

Directions:

To make the marinara sauce

1. In a saucepan over medium-low heat, warm the olive oil, then add the garlic and sauté for 1 to 2 minutes, until fragrant.
2. Add the tomatoes and simmer for 8 minutes, stirring occasionally. Keep warm until ready to use.

To make the eggplant bites

1. Preheat the air fryer to 370°F.
2. Toss the eggplant cubes in the olive oil.
3. Coat the eggplant cubes in the panko bread crumbs.
4. Place the eggplant in a single layer in the air fryer basket and cook for 9 minutes, shaking or stirring halfway through.
5. Cook for another 1 minute, until golden brown. Serve the eggplant bites with the marinara sauce on the side for dipping.

Nutrition:

Calories: 224	Carbs: 24g	Sodium: 70mg
Fat: 14g	Protein: 4g	Potassium: 374mg

150. Broccoli Salad

Preparation time: 10 minutes   Cooking time: 15 minutes   Servings: 2

Ingredients:

- 5 slices bacon
- 1/2 cup fresh broccoli, chopped
- 1/8 cup red onion, minced
- 1/4 cup raisins
- 1 1/2 tbsp. white wine vinegar
- 1/2 cup mayonnaise

Directions:

1. Cook the bacon in a frying pan over medium heat until crispy. Drain, crumble, and set aside.
2. In a medium bowl, combine broccoli, onion, and raisins.
3. In a small bowl, mix white wine vinegar and mayonnaise. Pour over the broccoli mixture and mix well.
4. Refrigerate for at least 2 hours to allow the flavors to meld.
5. Before serving, mix the salad with the crumbled bacon.

Nutrition:

Calories: 233	Carbs: 14g	Sodium: 316mg
Fat: 18g	Protein: 6g	Potassium: 253mg

151.   Kale, Quinoa, and Avocado Salad

Preparation time: 5 minutes   Cooking time: 25 minutes   Servings: 2

Ingredients:

- 1/3 cup quinoa
- 2/3 cup water
- 1/2 bunch kale, torn into bite-sized pieces
- 1/4 avocado, peeled, diced, and pitted
- 1/4 cup cucumber, chopped
- 1/4 cup red pepper, chopped
- 1 tbsp. red onion, chopped

Directions:

1. Boil the quinoa and 2/3 cup of water in a pan. Adjust heat and simmer until quinoa is tender and water is absorbed for about 15 to 20 minutes. Set aside to cool.
2. Place the kale in a steam basket over more than an inch of boiling water in a pan. Seal the pan with a lid and steam until hot, about 45 seconds; transfer to a large plate. Top with quinoa, avocado, cucumber, red pepper, and red onion.

Nutrition:

Calories: 189   Carbs: 32g   Sodium: 37mg
Fat: 6g   Protein: 7g   Potassium: 551mg

152.   Garden Salad

Preparation time: 5 minutes   Cooking time: 20 minutes   Servings: 2

Ingredients:

- 1/2 lb. raw peanuts in the shell
- 1 medium-sized tomato, chopped
- 1/4 cup green pepper, diced
- 1/4 cup sweet onion, diced
- 1/4 cup celery, diced
- 1 tbsp. olive oil
- 1/2 tsp. flavored vinegar

Directions:

1. Boil peanuts for 1 minute and rinse them.
2. Discard the softened peanut skins.
3. In a large bowl, combine the peanuts, diced tomato, green pepper, sweet onion, and celery.
4. In another bowl, whisk together olive oil and flavored vinegar.
5. Pour the mixture over the salad and mix well.

Nutrition:

Calories: 232   Carbs: 10g   Sodium: 18mg
Protein: 10g   Fat: 18g   Potassium: 369mg

153.   Baked Smoky Broccoli and Garlic

Preparation time: 5 minutes   Cooking time: 20 minutes   Servings: 2

Ingredients:

- 1 tsp. extra-virgin olive oil
- 1 clove garlic, minced
- 1/8 tsp. sea salt
- 1/8 tsp. black pepper, ground
- 1/4 tsp. cumin
- 1 3/4 cups broccoli, sliced

Directions:

1. Preheat your oven to 450F.
2. Set a baking sheet with foil and grease with olive oil.
3. Mix the olive oil, garlic, cumin, salt, and pepper in a bowl.
4. Add in the broccoli and combine until well coated.
5. Arrange in a single layer on the baking sheet.
6. Roast in the oven until vegetables become caramelized, for about 25 minutes.

Nutrition:

Calories: 64   Carbs: 6.8g   Sodium: 123mg
Protein: 2.9g   Fat: 3.6g   Potassium: 322mg

154. Roasted Cauliflower and Lima Beans

Preparation time: 5 minutes   Cooking time: 20 minutes   Servings: 2

Ingredients:

- 1/2 tbsp. vegan butter/margarine, melted
- 3 cloves garlic, minced
- 1/8 tsp. sea salt
- 1/8 tsp. black pepper, ground
- 3/4 cup cauliflower, sliced
- 1 cup cherry tomatoes
- 1/2 (15 oz.) can lima beans, drained

Directions:

1. Preheat your oven to 450F.
2. Set a baking sheet with foil and grease with melted vegan butter or margarine.
3. Mix the vegan butter, garlic, salt, and pepper in a bowl.
4. Add in the cauliflower, tomatoes, and lima beans.
5. Combine until well coated.
6. Set them out in a single layer on the baking sheet.
7. Roast in the oven until vegetables become caramelized, for about 25 minutes.

Nutrition:

Calories: 154	Carbs: 20.1g	Sodium: 263mg
Protein: 6.5g	Fat: 6.1g	Potassium: 752mg

155. Cauliflower Salad with Tahini Vinaigrette

Preparation time: 15 minutes   Cooking time: 5 minutes   Servings: 2

Ingredients:

- 1 1/2 lb. cauliflower
- 3 tbsp. lemon juice
- 1 tsp. olive oil
- 1/2 cup parsley, chopped
- 1/4 tsp. salt
- 1/4 cup shallot, chopped
- 2 tbsp. tahini

Directions:

1. Grate the cauliflower in a microwave-safe container. Add olive oil and salt. Be sure to cover and season the cauliflower evenly. Wrap the bowl with plastic wrap and heat it in the microwave for about 3 minutes.
2. Put the cauliflower on a baking sheet and let cool for about 10 minutes. Add the lemon juice and the shallots. Let it rest to allow the cauliflower to absorb the flavor.
3. In a separate bowl, mix tahini, parsley, and salt. Add this mixture to the cauliflower and mix everything well.

Nutrition:

Calories: 252	Carbs: 25.7g	Sodium: 402mg
Fat: 14.5g	Protein: 9.9g	Potassium: 1396mg

156. White Beans with Spinach and Pan-Roasted Tomatoes

Preparation time: 15 minutes   Cooking time: 10 minutes   Servings: 2

Ingredients:

- 1 tbsp. olive oil
- 4 small plum tomatoes, halved lengthwise
- 10 oz. spinach, frozen, defrosted and squeezed of excess water
- 2 garlic cloves, thinly sliced
- 1/4 tsp. black pepper, freshly ground
- 1 can white beans, drained (about 1 1/2 cups)
- Juice of 1 lemon

Directions:

1. Heat the oil in a large skillet over medium-high heat. Place the tomatoes, cut-side down, and cook for 3 to 5 minutes; turn and cook for 1 minute more. Transfer to a plate.
2. Reduce heat to medium and add the spinach, garlic, pepper to the skillet. Cook, tossing until the spinach is heated through, 2 to 3 minutes.
3. Return the tomatoes to the skillet, add the white beans and lemon juice, and toss until heated through, 1 to 2 minutes.

Nutrition:

Calories: 420	Carbs: 63g	Sodium: 405mg
Fat: 9g	Protein: 25g	Potassium: 1780mg

157.   Bean Hummus

Preparation time: 10 minutes   Cooking time: 40 minutes   Servings: 2

Ingredients:

- 1/2 cup chickpeas, soaked
- 3 cups of water
- 1/2 tablespoon tahini paste
- 1 garlic clove
- 2 tbsp olive oil
- 2 tbsp lemon juice
- 1/2 teaspoon harissa

Directions:

1. Pour water into the saucepan. Add chickpeas and close the lid.
2. Cook the chickpeas for 40 minutes on low heat or until they are soft.
3. After this, transfer the cooked chickpeas to the food processor.
4. Add olive oil, harissa, lemon juice, garlic clove, and tahini paste.
5. Blend the hummus until it is smooth.

Nutrition:

Calories: 256   Carbs: 25g   Sodium: 20mg

Fat: 15g   Protein: 8g   Potassium: 325mg

158.   Hasselback Eggplant

Preparation time: 15 minutes   Cooking time: 25 minutes   Servings: 2

Ingredients:

- 1 large eggplant, trimmed
- 1 large tomato, sliced
- 1 tablespoon low-fat yogurt
- 1 teaspoon curry powder
- 1 teaspoon olive oil

Directions:

1. Make Hasselback cuts in the eggplant.
2. Spread the eggplant with curry powder and fill with sliced tomatoes.
3. Drizzle the eggplant with olive oil and yogurt, and wrap it in foil.
4. Bake at 375°F for 25 minutes.

Nutrition:

Calories: 164   Carbs: 30g   Sodium: 25mg

Fat: 4g   Protein: 5g   Potassium: 977mg

159.   Black-Eyed Peas and Greens Power Salad

Preparation time: 15 minutes   Cooking time: 6 minutes   Servings: 2

Ingredients:

- 1 tablespoon olive oil
- 1 1/2 cups purple cabbage, chopped
- 2 1/2 cups baby spinach
- 1 cup carrots, shredded
- 1/2 can black-eyed peas, drained
- Juice of 1/2 lemon
- Salt and black pepper, to taste

Directions:

1. In a medium pan, add oil and cabbage, and sauté for 1 to 2 minutes on medium heat. Add spinach, cover for 3 to 4 minutes on medium heat, until greens are wilted. Remove from heat and add to a large bowl.
2. Add carrots, black-eyed peas, and a splash of lemon juice. Season with salt and pepper, if desired. Toss and serve.

Nutrition:

Calories: 238   Carbs: 33g   Sodium: 135mg

Fat: 8g   Protein: 10g   Potassium: 890mg

160.   Butternut-Squash Macaroni and Cheese

Preparation time: 15 minutes   Cooking time: 20 minutes   Servings: 2

Ingredients:

- 1/2 cup whole-wheat ziti macaroni
- 1 cup butternut squash, peeled and cubed
- 1/2 cup non-fat or low-fat milk, divided
- 1 teaspoon Dijon mustard
- 1 tablespoon olive oil
- 1/4 cup low-fat cheddar cheese, shredded

Directions:

1. Cook the pasta al dente. Place the butternut squash and 1/4 cup milk in a medium saucepan over medium-high heat. Season with black pepper. Bring to a simmer, lower the heat, and cook until fork-tender, 8 to 10 minutes.
2. Add squash and Dijon mustard to a blender. Purée until smooth. In a sauté pan, add olive oil. Add the squash purée and the remaining 1/4 cup of milk. Simmer for 5 minutes. Add the cheese and stir to combine.
3. Add the pasta to the sauté pan and stir to combine. Serve immediately.

Nutrition:

Calories: 349   Carbs: 42g   Sodium: 193mg

Fat: 15g   Protein: 15g   Potassium: 602mg

161.   Healthy Vegetable Fried Rice

Preparation time: 15 minutes   Cooking time: 10 minutes   Servings: 2

Ingredients:

- 1/2 cup brown rice, cooked
- 1/2 cup mixed vegetables, frozen
- 1/2 cup edamame, frozen
- 1 large egg, slightly beaten
- 1 tsp olive oil
- 1 tbsp garlic vinegar
- 1 tsp dark molasses

Directions:

1. Combine garlic vinegar and molasses in a small bowl.
2. Heat olive oil in a large skillet over medium-high heat. Add the egg and cook until set, about 1 minute. Break up the egg into small pieces with a spatula or spoon.
3. Add frozen mixed vegetables and edamame. Cook for 4 minutes, stirring frequently.
4. Add cooked brown rice and the vinegar-molasses mixture to the skillet. Cook for 5 minutes, stirring occasionally, until heated through. Serve immediately.

Nutrition:

Calories: 245   Carbs: 36g   Sodium: 50mg

Fat: 6g   Protein: 11g   Potassium: 355mg

162.   Carrot Cakes

Preparation time: 10 minutes   Cooking time: 10 minutes   Servings: 2

Ingredients:

- 1/2 cup grated carrot
- 1/2 tablespoon semolina
- 1/2 large egg, beaten
- 1/2 teaspoon Italian seasonings
- 1/2 tablespoon sesame oil

Directions:

1. In a bowl, mix grated carrot, semolina, egg, and Italian seasonings.
2. Heat sesame oil in a skillet.
3. Form carrot cakes with 2 spoons and place them in the skillet.
4. Cook the cakes for 4 minutes per side.

Nutrition:

Calories: 128   Carbs: 16g   Sodium: 45mg

Fat: 4g   Protein: 4g   Potassium: 161mg

163.   Vegan Chili

Preparation time: 10 minutes   Cooking time: 25 minutes   Servings: 2

Ingredients:

- 1/4 cup bulgur
- 1/2 cup chopped tomatoes
- 1/2 chili pepper, chopped
- 1/2 cup cooked red kidney beans
- 1 cup low-sodium vegetable broth
- 1/2 teaspoon tomato paste
- 1/4 cup chopped celery stalk

Directions:

1. Combine all ingredients in a medium saucepan and stir well.
2. Cover and simmer the chili for 25 minutes over medium-low heat.

Nutrition:

Calories: 166   Carbs: 33g   Sodium: 34mg
Fat: 1g   Protein: 8g   Potassium: 583mg

164.   Aromatic Whole Grain Spaghetti

Preparation time: 5 minutes   Cooking time: 10 minutes   Servings: 2

Ingredients:

- 3 oz. whole-grain spaghetti
- 1 cup water
- 1/8 cup soy milk
- 1/2 teaspoon dried basil
- 1/2 teaspoon ground nutmeg

Directions:

1. Bring water to a boil, then add spaghetti and cook for 8-10 minutes.
2. Meanwhile, heat soy milk in a small saucepan.
3. Drain cooked pasta and combine with ground nutmeg, soy milk, and dried basil in a mixing bowl.
4. Stir well and serve.

Nutrition:

Calories: 185   Carbs: 36g   Sodium: 19mg
Fat: 2g   Protein: 8g   Potassium: 130mg

165.   Chunky Tomatoes

Preparation time: 5 minutes   Cooking time: 15 minutes   Servings: 2

Ingredients:

- 1 cup plum tomatoes, roughly chopped
- 1/4 cup onion, diced
- 1/4 teaspoon garlic, minced
- 1/2 teaspoon Italian seasonings
- 1/2 teaspoon canola oil
- 1/2 chili pepper, chopped

Directions:

1. Heat canola oil in a saucepan.
2. Add chili pepper and onion. Cook the vegetables for 5 minutes, stirring occasionally.
3. Add tomatoes, garlic, and Italian seasonings.
4. Cover and sauté for 10 minutes.

Nutrition:

Calories: 52   Carbs: 10g   Sodium: 17mg
Fat: 1g   Protein: 2g   Potassium: 276mg

166.   Baby minted carrots

Preparation time: 35 minutes   Cooking time: 20 minutes   Servings: 2

Ingredients:

- 2 cups water
- 1/3 pound baby carrots, rinsed (about 1 2/3 cups)
- 1/8 cup 100% apple juice
- 1/2 tablespoon cornstarch
- 1/4 tablespoon chopped fresh mint leaves
- 1/16 teaspoon ground cinnamon

Directions:

1. In a large saucepan, bring the water to a boil. Add the carrots and cook for about 10 minutes, until tender-crisp. Drain the carrots and place them in a serving bowl.
2. In a small saucepan over medium heat, combine the apple juice and cornstarch. Cook for about 5 minutes, stirring until the mixture thickens. Stir in the cinnamon and mint.
3. Pour the mixture over the carrots and serve immediately.

Nutrition:

Calories: 55	Carbs: 12.5g	Sodium: 46mg
Fat: 0.1g	Protein: 1g	Potassium: 292mg

167.   Baked Falafel

Preparation time: 10 minutes   Cooking time: 25 minutes   Servings: 2

Ingredients:

- 2/3 cup chickpeas, cooked
- 1/4 yellow onion, diced
- 1 tablespoon olive oil
- 1/3 cup fresh parsley, chopped
- 1/3 teaspoon ground cumin
- 1/8 teaspoon coriander
- 1 garlic clove, diced

Directions:

1. Add all ingredients to a blender and blend until smooth.
2. Preheat the oven to 375°F (190°C).
3. Line a baking sheet with parchment paper.
4. Make balls with the chickpea mixture and gently press them into a falafel shape.
5. Place the falafel on the baking sheet and bake for 25 minutes.

Nutrition:

Calories: 213	Carbs: 25g	Sodium: 14mg
Fat: 10g	Protein: 8g	Potassium: 112mg

168.   Paella

Preparation time: 10 min   Cooking time: 25 min   Servings: 2

Ingredients:

- 1/2 teaspoon dried saffron
- 1/2 cup short-grain rice
- 1/2 tablespoon olive oil
- 1 cup water
- 1/2 teaspoon chili flakes
- 2 oz. artichoke hearts, chopped
- 1/4 cup green peas

Directions:

1. Pour water into a saucepan, add rice, and cook for 15 minutes.
2. Meanwhile, heat olive oil in a skillet.
3. Add chili flakes, dried saffron, and artichoke hearts. Cook the vegetables for 5 minutes.
4. Combine the cooked rice with the vegetable mixture.
5. Add green peas, stir well, and cook for an additional 10 minutes over low heat.

Nutrition:

Calories: 276	Carbs: 47g	Sodium: 15mg
Fat: 7g	Protein: 7g	Potassium: 254mg

169.   Mushroom Cakes

Preparation time: 15 minutes   Cooking time: 10 minutes   Servings: 2

Ingredients:

- 1 cup mushrooms, chopped
- 1 1/2 garlic cloves, chopped
- 1/2 tablespoon dried dill
- 1/2 egg, beaten
- 1/8 cup of rice, cooked
- 1/2 tablespoon sesame oil
- 1/2 teaspoon chili powder

Directions:
1. Grind the mushrooms in a food processor.
2. Add the egg, rice, garlic, dill, and chili powder.
3. Blend the mixture for 10 seconds.
4. Heat up sesame oil for 1 minute.
5. Make medium-sized mushroom cakes and put them in the hot sesame oil.
6. Cook the mushroom cakes for 10 minutes (about 5 minutes per side) on medium heat.

Nutrition:

Calories: 155	Carbs: 13g	Sodium: 15mg
Fat: 8g	Protein: 6g	Potassium: 308mg

170. Glazed Eggplant Rings

Preparation time: 10 minutes   Cooking time: 10 minutes   Servings: 2

Ingredients:
- 1 1/2 eggplants, sliced
- 1/2 tablespoon liquid honey
- 1/2 teaspoon minced ginger
- 1 tablespoon lemon juice
- 1 1/2 tablespoons avocado oil
- 1/4 teaspoon ground coriander
- 1 1/2 tablespoons water

Directions:
1. Rub the eggplants with ground coriander.
2. Heat the avocado oil in a skillet for 1 minute.
3. When the oil is hot, add the sliced eggplant and arrange it in one layer.
4. Cook the vegetables for 2 minutes per side.
5. Transfer the eggplant to a bowl.
6. Add liquid honey, minced ginger, lemon juice, and water to the skillet.
7. Bring it to a boil and then add cooked eggplants.
8. Coat the vegetables in the sweet liquid well and cook for another 2 minutes..

Nutrition:

Calories: 225	Carbs: 26g	Sodium: 25mg
Fat: 14g	Protein: 3g	Potassium: 756mg

171. Sweet Potato Balls

Preparation time: 15 minutes   Cooking time: 10 minutes   Servings: 2

Ingredients:
- 1/2 cup sweet potato, mashed, cooked
- 1/2 tablespoon fresh cilantro, chopped
- 1/2 egg, beaten
- 1 1/2 tablespoons ground oatmeal
- 1/2 teaspoon ground paprika
- 1/4 teaspoon ground turmeric
- 1 tablespoon coconut oil

Directions:
1. Mix mashed sweet potato, paprika, fresh cilantro, egg, ground oatmeal, and turmeric in a bowl.
2. Stir the mixture until smooth and form small balls.
3. Heat the coconut oil in a saucepan.
4. When the coconut oil is hot, add the sweet potato balls.
5. Cook them until golden brown.

Nutrition:

Calories: 165	Carbs: 20g	Sodium: 25mg
Fat: 8g	Protein: 4g	Potassium: 344mg

172.   Chickpea Curry

Preparation time: 10 minutes   Cooking time: 10 minutes   Servings: 2

Ingredients:

- 3/4 cup chickpeas, boiled
- 1/2 teaspoon curry powder
- 1/4 teaspoon garam masala
- 1/2 cup spinach, chopped
- 1/2 teaspoon coconut oil
- 1/8 cup of soy milk
- 1/2 tablespoon tomato paste

Directions:

1. Heat coconut oil in a saucepan.
2. Add tomato paste, curry powder, garam masala, and soy milk.
3. Stir the mixture until smooth and bring it to a boil.
4. Add spinach and chickpeas.
5. Stir the meal and close the lid.
6. Cook it for 5 minutes over medium-high heat.

Nutrition:

Calories: 170   Carbs: 23g   Sodium: 24mg
Fat: 5g   Protein: 8g   Potassium: 277mg

173.   Quinoa Bowl

Preparation time: 15 minutes   Cooking time: 15 minutes   Servings: 2

Ingredients:

- 1/2 cup quinoa
- 1 cup of water
- 1/2 cup tomatoes, diced
- 1/2 cup sweet pepper, diced
- 1/4 cup of rice, cooked
- 1/2 tablespoon lemon juice
- 1/4 teaspoon lemon zest, grated

Directions:

1. Mix quinoa and water and cook it for 15 minutes. After this, remove it from the heat and let it rest for 10 minutes.
2. Transfer the cooked quinoa to a big bowl.
3. Add tomatoes, rice, lemon juice, sweet pepper, and lemon zest.
4. Stir the mixture well and transfer it to serving bowls.

Nutrition:

Calories: 235   Carbs: 46g   Sodium: 34mg
Fat: 3g   Protein: 8g   Potassium: 175mg

174.   Vegan Meatloaf

Preparation time: 10 minutes   Cooking time: 30 minutes   Servings: 2

Ingredients:

- 1/2 cup chickpeas, cooked
- 1/2 onion, diced
- 1/2 tablespoon ground flax seeds
- 1/4 teaspoon chili flakes
- 1/2 tablespoon coconut oil
- 1/4 cup carrot, diced
- 1/4 cup celery stalk, chopped

Directions:

1. Heat coconut oil in a saucepan.
2. Add onion, carrot, and celery stalk. Cook the vegetables for 10 minutes.
3. Then add chili flakes, chickpeas, and ground flax seeds.
4. Blend the mixture until smooth with an immersion blender.
5. Line a small loaf mold with baking paper and transfer the blended mixture inside.
6. Flatten well.
7. Bake the meatloaf in the preheated to 365°F oven for 22 minutes.

Nutrition:

Calories: 225   Carbs: 31g   Sodium: 30mg
Fat: 8g   Protein: 9g   Potassium: 178mg

175.   Loaded Potato Skins

Preparation time: 15 minutes   Cooking time: 45 minutes   Servings: 2

Ingredients:

- 2 potatoes
- 1/3 teaspoon ground black pepper
- 2 teaspoons olive oil
- 1/6 teaspoon minced garlic
- 1/8 cup of soy milk

Directions:

1. Preheat the oven to 400°F.
2. Pierce the potatoes with a fork 2-3 times and bake for 30 minutes or until tender.
3. After this, cut the baked potatoes into halves and scoop out the potato flesh into a bowl.
4. Drizzle the scooped potato halves with olive oil and ground black pepper and return to the oven. Bake them until they are light brown.
5. Mash the scooped potato flesh and mix it with soy milk and minced garlic.
6. Fill the cooked potato halves with the mashed potato mixture.

Nutrition:

Calories: 170   Carbs: 28g   Sodium: 25.5mg

Fat: 4g   Protein: 5g   Potassium: 108mg

14. Desserts

176.   Banana-Cashew Cream Mousse

Preparation time: 55 minutes   Cooking time: 0 minutes   Servings: 2

Ingredients:

- 1/2 cup cashews, presoaked
- 1 tablespoon honey
- 1 teaspoon vanilla extract
- 1 large banana, sliced (reserve 4 slices for garnish)
- 1 cup plain nonfat Greek yogurt

Directions:

1. Set the cashews in a small bowl and cover with 1 cup of water.
2. Soak at room temperature for 2 to 3 hours.
3. Drain, rinse, and set aside.
4. Place honey, vanilla extract, cashews, and bananas in a blender or food processor.
5. Blend until smooth.
6. Place mixture in a medium bowl.
7. Fold in yogurt, mix well. Cover.
8. Chill in refrigerator, covered, for at least 45 minutes.
9. Portion mousse into 2 serving bowls. Garnish each with 2 banana slices.

Nutrition:

Calories: 329   Carbs: 45g   Sodium: 64mg

Fat: 14g   Protein: 17g   Potassium: 107mg

177.   Cherry Stew

Preparation time: 10 minutes   Cooking time: 10 minutes   Servings: 2

Ingredients:

- 2/3 cup cherries, pitted
- 1/8 cup cocoa powder
- 1/8 cup coconut sugar
- 2/3 cup water

Directions:

1. In a pan, combine the cherries with the water, sugar, and cocoa powder, stir, cook over medium heat for 10 minutes.
2. Divide into bowls and serve cold.

Nutrition:

Calories: 143   Carbs: 35g   Sodium: 7mg

Fat: 2g   Protein: 2g   Potassium: 60mg

178.   Sriracha Parsnip Fries

Preparation time: 10 minutes   Cooking time: 25 minutes   Servings: 2

Ingredients:

- 1/2 pound parsnips, peeled, cut into 3 × 1/2-inch strips
- 1/2 tablespoon olive oil
- 1/2 teaspoon dried rosemary
- Sriracha to taste
- Salt and pepper to taste

Directions:

1. Preheat oven to 450°F. Mix parsnips, rosemary, and oil in a medium size bowl.
2. Season with salt, pepper, and sriracha to taste and toss to coat.
3. Lay parsnips on a baking sheet, ensuring the strips don't overlap. Bake for 10 minutes.
4. Turn and roast until parsnips are browned in spots, 10 to 15 minutes longer.
5. If you want them to be extra crispy, turn the broiler on for the last 2 to 3 minutes.

Nutrition:

Calories: 115   Carbs: 17g   Sodium: 8mg

Fat: 4g   Protein: 1g   Potassium: 64mg

179.   Tortilla Strawberry Chips

Preparation time: 10 minutes   Cooking time: 25 minutes   Servings: 2

Ingredients:

- 5 strawberries, sliced
- 1/4 tsp. cayenne
- 1 tbsp. organic extra virgin olive oil
- 4 small whole wheat grain tortillas
- 1/2 tbsp. chili powder

Directions:

1. Preheat oven to 350°F.
2. Spread the tortillas on the lined baking sheet. Drizzle with olive oil and sprinkle with chili powder and cayenne.
3. Distribute the sliced strawberries evenly across the tortillas.
4. Bake for 25 minutes, or until tortillas are crispy.
5. Remove from oven, let cool, then cut into chips.

Nutrition:

Calories: 228   Carbs: 33g   Sodium: 308mg
Fat: 9g   Protein: 5g   Potassium: 179mg

180.   Almond Rice Pudding

Preparation time: 10 minutes   Cooking time: 30 minutes   Servings: 2

Ingredients:

- 1/8 cup sugar
- 1/2 tsp. vanilla
- 1 1/2 cup milk (use low-fat or fat-free milk for DASH compliance)
- 1/2 cup white rice
- 1/8 cup toasted almonds
- Cinnamon, as required

Directions:

1. In a pan, combine the milk and rice, and bring to a boil. Lower the heat and let it simmer, covered, for 30 minutes, or until the rice is tender.
2. Remove from heat and add sugar, vanilla, and a sprinkle of cinnamon. Mix well.
3. Divide the pudding into two bowls and garnish with toasted almonds before serving.

Nutrition:

Calories: 340   Carbs: 58g   Sodium: 85mg
Fat: 8g   Protein: 10g   Potassium: 337mg

181.   Sweet Potatoes and Apples Mix

Preparation Time: 10 minutes   Cooking Time: 1 hour and 10 minutes   Servings: 1

Ingredients:

- 1/2 tbsp. low-fat butter
- 1/4 lb. cored and chopped apples
- 1 tbsp. water
- 1 lb. sweet potatoes

Directions:

1. Preheat the oven to 400°F. Place the sweet potatoes on a lined baking sheet and bake for 1 hour, or until tender. Once baked, peel and mash the sweet potatoes.
2. In a pot, add apples and water. Bring to a boil over medium heat, then reduce heat and cook for 10 minutes, until apples are tender.
3. Transfer the cooked apples to a bowl and add the mashed sweet potatoes. Stir well to combine.
4. Serve the mixture in a bowl and enjoy!

Nutrition:

Calories: 507   Carbs: 107g   Sodium: 46mg
Fat: 6g   Protein: 6g   Potassium: 1748mg

182.   Sautéed Bananas with Orange Sauce

Preparation time: 5 minutes   Cooking time: 5 minutes   Servings: 2

Ingredients:

- 2 tbsp frozen pure orange juice concentrate
- 1 tbsp margarine
- 1/8 cup sliced almonds
- 1/2 tsp orange zest
- 1/2 tsp fresh grated ginger
- 2 firm, sliced ripe bananas
- 1/2 tsp cinnamon

Directions:

1. Melt the margarine over medium heat in a large skillet until it bubbles but before it begins to brown.
2. Add the cinnamon, ginger, and orange zest. Cook, while stirring, for 1 minute before adding the orange juice concentrate.
3. Cook, while stirring, until an even sauce has formed.
4. Add the bananas and cook, stirring carefully for 1-2 minutes, or until warmed and evenly coated with the sauce.
5. Serve warm with sliced almonds.

Nutrition:

Calories: 270   Carbs: 41g   Sodium: 99mg

Fat: 12g   Protein: 3g   Potassium: 597mg

183.   Caramelized Blood Oranges with Ginger Cream

Preparation time: 10 minutes   Cooking time: 15 minutes   Servings: 2

Ingredients:

- 1 tbsp low sugar orange marmalade
- 1 1/2 tsp divided fresh grated ginger
- 2 cups peeled and sliced blood oranges
- 1 tbsp brown sugar
- 1/4 cup coconut cream

Directions:

1. Preheat the broiler.
2. In a small saucepan, combine the orange marmalade and 1 tsp of fresh ginger. Heat over low heat and stir until the mixture becomes slightly liquefied.
3. Place a thin layer of the oranges into the bottom of two large baking ramekins and brush with the marmalade mixture. Repeat this step until all of the oranges have been used. Pour any remaining gingered marmalade over the tops of the ramekins.
4. Sprinkle each ramekin with brown sugar and place under the broiler for approximately 5 minutes, or until caramelized.
5. Serve warm garnished with coconut cream.

Nutrition:

Calories: 234   Carbs: 35g   Sodium: 26mg

Protein: 2.3g   Fat: 10g   Potassium: 337mg

184.   Grilled Minted Watermelon

Preparation time: 10 minutes   Cooking time: 10 minutes   Servings: 2

Ingredients:

- 1/2 tbsp honey
- 2 tbsp finely chopped fresh mint
- 4 thick deseeded watermelon slices

Directions:

1. Prepare and preheat a stovetop grill.
2. Lightly press towels against the watermelon slices to remove as much excess moisture as possible.
3. Lightly brush both sides of the watermelon slices with honey.
4. Place the watermelon slices on the grill and grill for approximately 3 minutes per side, or until slightly caramelized.
5. Serve warm, sprinkled with fresh mint.

Nutrition:

Calories: 107   Carbs: 26g   Sodium: 8.3mg

Protein: 1.3g   Fat: 1g   Potassium: 232mg

185.   Caramelized Apricot Pots

Preparation time: 10 minutes   Cooking time: 5 minutes   Servings: 2

Ingredients:

- 1 tbsp white sugar
- 1 tsp lemon juice
- 1/4 tsp thyme
- 1 cup sliced apricots
- 1 tsp brown sugar
- 1/3 cup part-skim ricotta cheese
- 1/2 tsp lemon zest

Directions:

1. Preheat the broiler of your oven.
2. Place the apricots in a bowl and toss with the lemon juice.
3. In another bowl, combine the ricotta cheese, thyme, and lemon zest. Mix well.
4. Spread a layer of the ricotta mixture into the bottoms of 2 large baking ramekins.
5. Spoon the apricots over the top of the ricotta cheese in each.
6. Combine the white sugar and brown sugar. Sprinkle evenly over the apricots, avoiding large clumps of sugar as much as possible.
7. Place the ramekins under the broiler for approximately 5 minutes, or until caramelized.
8. Serve warm.

Nutrition:

Calories: 202   Carbs: 35g   Protein: 6g
Fat: 5g   Sodium: 55mg   Potassium: 265mg

186.   Pumpkin Pie

Preparation time: 15 minutes   Cooking time: 45 minutes   Servings: 2

Ingredients:

- 1/4 cup ginger cookies
- 1/2 cup canned pumpkin, pureed
- 1/8 cup egg whites
- 1/8 cup sugar
- 1/2 teaspoon pumpkin pie spice
- 1/4 cup evaporated skim milk
- 1/2 teaspoon ground cinnamon

Directions:

1. Add cookies to a food processor and blitz until coarsely chopped.
2. Preheat the oven to 350°F and coat a small springform pan with cooking spray.
3. Spread the crumbled cookies onto the bottom of the pan and press into the bottom.
4. Mix pumpkin, egg whites, sugar, milk, pumpkin pie spice, and cinnamon in a bowl.
5. Pour the mixture on the crust and bake for 45 minutes.
6. Let cool slightly before serving.

Nutrition:

Calories: 228   Sodium: 84mg   Protein: 7g
Fat: 4g   Carbs: 42g   Potassium: 281mg

187.   Chocolate Avocado Mousse

Preparation time: 5 minutes   Cooking time: 5 minutes   Servings: 2

Ingredients:

- 1/2 avocado
- 2 tbsp almond milk
- 2 tbsp cacao powder
- 1/2 teaspoon vanilla extract
- 1 tablespoon coconut oil

Directions:

1. Add all ingredients to a blender and blitz until smooth.
2. Divide the mixture among two ramekins, cover and refrigerate for at least 1-2 hours.
3. Serve.

Nutrition:

Calories: 248	Protein: 3g	Sodium: 12mg
Carbs: 12g	Fat: 22g	Potassium: 284mg

188.　　Lemon Cheesecake

Preparation time: 5 minutes　　　　Cooking time: 10 minutes　　　　Servings: 2

Ingredients:

- 1 cup low-fat cottage cheese
- 1/4 cup skim milk
- 1 egg white
- 2 tbsp sugar
- 1/2 tsp vanilla
- 1 tbsp cold water
- 1/2 envelope unflavored gelatin
- 1 tbsp lemon juice

Directions:

1. Mix water, gelatin, and lemon juice in a bowl.
2. Let rest until gelatin softens. Add milk to a saucepan and heat until almost boiling.
3. Add gelatin mixture and stir until dissolved. Add egg white, vanilla, sugar, and cottage cheese.
4. Blend the mixture until smooth.
5. Pour the batter into a small dish and refrigerate for 2-3 hours.
6. Serve topped with lemon zest.

Nutrition:

Calories: 233	Carbs: 27g	Sodium: 508mg
Protein: 14.35g	Fat: 10.55g	Potassium: 56mg

189.　　Apple and Almond Muffins

Preparation time: 10 minutes　　　　Cooking time: 20 minutes　　　　Servings: 2

Ingredients:

- 2 ounces ground almonds
- 1/2 teaspoon cinnamon
- 1/4 teaspoon baking powder
- 1 pinch sunflower seeds
- 1/2 whole egg
- 1/2 teaspoon apple cider vinegar
- 1 tablespoon Erythritol
- 2 1/2 tablespoons apple sauce

Directions:

1. Preheat your oven to 350°F. Line a muffin tin with 2 paper muffin cups and set aside.
2. In a bowl, combine ground almonds, cinnamon, baking powder, and sunflower seeds. Set aside.
3. In another bowl, whisk together the egg, apple cider vinegar, apple sauce, and Erythritol.
4. Add the wet mixture to the dry ingredients and mix well until you have a smooth batter.
5. Divide the batter evenly between the 2 muffin cups and bake for 20 minutes or until a toothpick inserted comes out clean.
6. Once baked, let the muffins cool before serving. Enjoy!

Nutrition:

Calories: 212	Carbs: 10 g	Sodium: 75 mg
Fat: 17 g	Protein: 7 g	Potassium: 110 mg

190.　　Toasted Almond Ambrosia

Preparation time: 10 minutes　　　　Cooking time: 20 minutes　　　　Servings: 2

Ingredients:

- 1/4 cup almonds, slivered
- 1/4 cup unsweetened shredded coconut
- 1 1/2 cups pineapple, cubed
- 2 oranges, segmented
- 1 red apple, cored and diced
- Fresh mint leaves for garnish (optional)

Directions:

1. Preheat your oven to 325°F and prepare a baking sheet.
2. Spread the almonds evenly on the baking sheet and roast for 10 minutes. Transfer them to a plate.
3. Toast the shredded coconut on the same baking sheet for 10 minutes.
4. In a bowl, mix together the pineapple, oranges, and apples.

5. Divide the fruit mixture between two serving bowls and top with toasted almonds and coconut. Garnish with mint leaves before serving (optional).

Nutrition:

Calories: 282	Carbs: 36g	Sodium: 9mg
Fat: 15g	Protein: 5g	Potassium: 625mg

191. Key Lime Cherry "Nice" Cream

Preparation time: 10 minutes   Cooking time: 15 minutes   Servings: 2

Ingredients:

- 2 frozen bananas, peeled
- 1/2 cup frozen dark sweet cherries
- Zest and juice of 1/2 lime, divided
- 1/4 teaspoon vanilla extract

Directions:

1. Place the bananas, cherries, lime juice, and vanilla extract in a food processor and purée until smooth, scraping the sides as needed.
2. Transfer the "nice" cream to bowls and top with the lime zest.

Nutrition:

Calories: 206	Carbs: 52g	Sodium: 3mg
Fat: 1g	Protein: 2g	Potassium: 737mg

192. Tart Raspberry Crumble Bar

Preparation time: 10 minutes   Cooking time: 45 minutes   Servings: 2

Ingredients:

- 1/4 cup whole toasted almonds
- 7/8 cup whole wheat flour
- 1/4 teaspoon salt
- 1/4 cup granulated sugar
- 9-ounce fresh raspberries
- 6 tablespoons cold, unsalted butter, sliced into cube

Directions:

1. Preheat the oven to 375°F and lightly grease a small baking pan with cooking spray.
2. In a food processor, pulse almonds until coarsely chopped. Transfer to a bowl.
3. Add flour, salt, and butter to the food processor and pulse until you have a coarse batter.
4. Divide the batter into two bowls. In the first bowl of batter, knead well until it forms a ball.
5. Press the dough evenly on the bottom of the pan.
6. Evenly spread raspberries over the dough.
7. In the second bowl of batter, add sugar. Pinch the batter to form clusters of streusels and top the raspberries with it.
8. Bake until golden brown and berries are bubbly, around 45 minutes.
9. Remove from oven and cool for 20 minutes before slicing into bars.

Nutrition:

Calories: 1004	Carbs: 119g	Sodium: 311mg
Protein: 13g	Fat: 54g	Potassium: 508mg

193. Easy Coconut-Carrot Cake Balls

Preparation time: 10 minutes   Cooking time: 0 minutes   Servings: 2

Ingredients:

- 1/4 cup peeled and finely shredded carrot
- 1/3 cup packed pitted medjool dates
- 1/2 cup raw walnuts
- 1/4 tsp. ground cinnamon
- 1 tsp. vanilla extract
- 2 tbsp. almond flour
- 2 tbsp. desiccated coconut flakes

Directions:

1. In a food processor, process dates until they form a clump.
2. Transfer to a bowl. In the same food processor, process walnuts and cinnamon until it resembles a fine meal.
3. Add the processed dates, vanilla extract, almond flour, and shredded carrots. Pulse until you form a loose dough but not mushy. Do not over-pulse.

4. Transfer to a bowl. Divide the carrot batter into 4 equal-sized balls.
5. Roll the balls in the coconut flakes, set in a lidded container, and refrigerate for 2 hours before enjoying.

Nutrition:

Calories: 340	Carbs: 27g	Sodium: 9mg
Protein: 7g	Fat: 24g	Potassium: 380mg

194. Apple Dumplings

Preparation Time: 10 minutes	Cooking Time: 30 minutes	Servings: 2

Ingredients:

Dough:

- 1/2 cup whole wheat flour
- 1 tablespoon butter
- 1 tablespoon honey, raw
- 3 tart apples, sliced thin

Directions:

1. Preheat the oven to 350°F.
2. In a food processor, mix the butter, flour, and honey until it forms a crumbly mixture.
3. Seal the dough in plastic and place it in the fridge for two hours.
4. Roll your dough into a sheet that's a quarter-inch thick. Cut out four-inch circles and place each circle into a greased muffin tray.
5. Press the dough down and stuff with the apple slices. Fold the edges and pinch them closed. Make sure they're well sealed.
6. Bake for 30 minutes until golden brown and serve drizzled with honey.

Nutrition:

Calories: 313	Carbs: 61g	Sodium: 39mg
Protein: 5g	Fat: 8g	Potassium: 260mg

195. Cauliflower Cinnamon Pudding

Preparation time: 10 minutes	Cooking time: 20 minutes	Servings: 2

Ingredients:

- 1/2 tbsp. coconut oil, melted
- 3.5 oz. cauliflower rice
- 8 oz. coconut milk
- 1.5 oz. coconut sugar
- 1/2 egg
- 1/2 tsp. cinnamon powder
- 1/2 tsp. vanilla extract

Directions:

1. In a pan, combine the oil with the cauliflower rice, coconut milk, coconut sugar, egg, cinnamon, and vanilla, whisk well, bring to a simmer, and cook for 20 minutes over medium heat.
2. Divide into bowls and serve cold.

Nutrition:

Calories: 304	Protein: 4g
Carbs: 34g	Sodium: 28mg
Fat: 18g	Potassium: 224mg

196. Coconut Mousse

Preparation time: 10 minutes	Cooking time: 0 minutes	Servings: 2

Ingredients:

- 1 cup coconut milk
- 1/2 teaspoon coconut extract
- 1/2 teaspoon vanilla extract
- 2 teaspoons coconut sugar
- 1/3 cup coconut, toasted

Directions:

1. In a bowl, combine the coconut milk with the coconut extract, vanilla extract, coconut sugar, and toasted coconut, whisk well.
2. Set into small cups and serve cold.

Nutrition:

Calories: 300	Fat: 28g	Protein: 3g
Carbs: 10g	Sodium: 19mg	Potassium: 284mg

197. Mango Pudding

Preparation time: 10 minutes   Cooking time: 50 minutes   Servings: 2

Ingredients:

- 1/2 cup brown rice
- 1 cup water
- 1/2 mango, peeled and chopped
- 1/2 cup coconut milk
- 1 tablespoon coconut sugar
- 1/2 teaspoon vanilla extract

Directions:

1. Put the water in a pan and bring to a boil over medium heat.
2. Add rice, stir, cover the pan, and cook for 40 minutes.
3. Add coconut milk, coconut sugar, vanilla extract, and chopped mango, stir, cover the pan again, and cook for 10 minutes more.
4. Divide into bowls and serve.

Nutrition:

Calories: 388	Fat: 14g	Sodium: 18mg
Carbs: 61g	Protein: 6g	Potassium: 376mg

198. Rhubarb Pie

Preparation time: 10 minutes   Cooking time: 25 minutes   Servings: 2

Ingredients:

- 1 cup whole wheat flour
- 1/4 cup low-fat butter, melted
- 1/4 cup pecans, chopped
- 1/2 cup coconut sugar, divided
- 1 cup rhubarb, chopped
- 1/2 cup strawberries, sliced

Directions:

1. In a bowl, combine the flour with the melted butter, pecans, and 1/4 cup coconut sugar, and stir well.
2. Transfer the mixture to a small pie pan, press well into the pan, and bake at 350°F for 20 minutes.
3. In a pan, combine the strawberries, rhubarb, and 1/4 cup coconut sugar, stir well, and cook over medium heat for 4 minutes.
4. Spread this over the pie crust and keep in the fridge for a few hours before slicing and serving.

Nutrition:

Calories: 556	Fat: 23g	Sodium: 97mg
Carbs: 84g	Protein: 9g	Potassium: 394mg

199. Fruit Skewers

Preparation time: 10 minutes   Cooking time: 0 minutes   Servings: 10

Ingredients:

- 2 strawberries, halved
- 1/4 cantaloupe, cubed
- 1 banana, cut into chunks
- 1 apple, cored and cut into chunks

Directions:

1. Thread strawberry, cantaloupe, banana, and apple chunks alternately onto skewers and serve them cold.
2. Enjoy!

Nutrition:

Calories: 89	Carbs: 22.9g	Sodium: 6.3mg
Protein: 1.2g	Fat: 0.5g	Potassium: 359mg

200. Pumpkin Pudding

Preparation time: 1 hour   Cooking time: 0 minutes   Servings: 2

Ingredients:

- 3/4 cup almond milk
- 1/4 cup pumpkin puree
- 1 tbsp. coconut sugar
- 1/4 tsp. cinnamon powder
- 1/8 tsp. ginger, grated
- 1/8 cup chia seeds

Directions:

1. In a bowl, combine the milk with pumpkin, sugar, cinnamon, ginger, and chia seeds, toss well, divide into small cups and keep them in the fridge for 1 hour before serving.
2. Enjoy!

Nutrition:

Calories: 155   Carbohydrates: 24.4g   Sodium: 58.5mg

Fat: 4.5g   Protein: 4.4g   Potassium: 161.4mg

201. Pop Corn Bites

Preparation time: 5 minutes   Cooking time: 2-3 minutes   Servings: 2

Ingredients:

- 1 cup Medjool dates, chopped
- 6 ounces brewed coffee
- 1/2 cup pecan, chopped
- 1/4 cup coconut, shredded
- 1/4 cup cocoa powder

Directions:

1. Dip dates in warm coffee for 5 minutes. Detach dates from coffee and mash them, making a fine smooth mixture.
2. Set in remaining ingredients (except cocoa powder) and form small balls out of the mixture. Coat with cocoa powder, serve and enjoy!

Nutrition:

Calories: 525   Sodium: 38mg   Protein: 5g

Fat: 28g   Carbs: 72g   Potassium: 99mg

202. Delicious Berry Pie

Preparation time: 10 minutes   Cooking time: 1 hour   Servings: 2

Ingredients:

- 1/4 cup whole wheat flour
- Cooking spray
- 1/6 cup almond milk
- 1/8 tsp. baking powder
- 1/8 tsp. stevia
- 1/8 cup blueberries
- 1/2 tsp. olive oil

Directions:

1. In a bowl, mix flour with baking powder, stevia, blueberries, milk, and oil, whisk.
2. Pour into a small, greased oven-safe dish.
3. Bake at 350°F for 25-30 minutes or until a toothpick comes out clean.
4. Let the pie cool down, slice, and serve.

Nutrition:

Calories: 110   Fat: 3g   Sodium: 28mg

Protein: 3g   Carbs: 18g   Potassium: 71mg

203. Gentle Sweet Potato Tempura

Preparation time: 10 minutes   Cooking time: 0 minutes   Servings: 2

Ingredients:

- 1 whole egg
- 1/8 teaspoon salt
- 1 cup oil (for frying)
- 1/2 cup ice water
- 1/2 sweet potato, scrubbed and sliced into 1/8-inch slices
- 1/2 cup all-purpose flour

Directions:
1. In a large bowl, beat the egg until frothy.
2. Stir in salt, ice water, and flour, mix well until the batter is lumpy.
3. In a frying pan over high heat, add oil and heat to 350°F.
4. Dry sweet potato slices and dip in the batter, letting excess batter drip. Fry until golden brown on both sides, about 2 minutes per side.
5. Remove and drain excess oil. Serve immediately.

Nutrition:

Calories: 134

Fat: 4.9g

Sodium: 27mg

Carbs: 12g

Protein: 3g

Potassium: 56.1mg

204.   Delightful Pizza Dip

Preparation time: 20 minutes

Cooking time: 0 minutes

Servings: 2

Ingredients:
- 1/2 cup pureed ripe tomato
- 1 ounce shredded Colby cheese
- 4 ounces Ricotta cheese
- 1/2 teaspoon garlic paste
- 1/4 teaspoon dried basil
- 1/4 teaspoon dried oregano
- 1/4 cup Kalamata olives, to garnish

Directions:
1. Preheat your oven to 360°F.
2. Combine tomato, Colby cheese, Ricotta cheese, garlic paste, dried basil, and dried oregano in a bowl.
3. Transfer the mixture to a small, oven-safe dish.
4. Top with Kalamata olives and bake for 15 minutes.
5. Serve hot and enjoy!

Nutrition:

Calories: 245

Fat: 18g

Sodium: 450mg

Carbs: 7g

Protein: 14g

Potassium: 212mg

205.   Strawberry Cheesecake

Preparation time: 4 hours

Cooking time: 0 minutes

Servings: 2

Ingredients:
- 1/2 cup crumbled graham crackers
- 2 tablespoons butter, melted
- 4 oz. cream cheese, softened
- 1/4 cup sour cream
- 1/4 lb. fresh strawberries, halved
- 3 tablespoons sugar
- 1/2 teaspoon vanilla extract

Directions:
1. Mix crackers and butter in a bowl. Prepare a small springform pan and coat with cooking spray.
2. Press the crust mixture into the bottom of the pan and refrigerate for 30 minutes. In a bowl, beat cream cheese and sugar until smooth.
3. Add sour cream and vanilla, stir well to combine.
4. Fold in strawberries. Set the mixture on top of the crust and refrigerate for about 3-4 hours.

Nutrition:

Calories: 617

Carbs: 60g

Sodium: 419mg

Fat: 41g

Protein: 8g

Potassium: 201mg

206.   Strawberries and Cream Cheese Crepes

Preparation time: 10 minutes

Cooking time: 10 minutes

Servings: 2

Ingredients:
- 2 tbsp. cream cheese, softened
- 1 tbsp. sifted powdered sugar
- 1 tsp. vanilla extract
- 1 prepackaged crepe, about 8 inches
- 4 strawberries, hulled and sliced
- 1/2 tsp. powdered sugar for garnish
- 1 tbsp. caramel sauce, warmed (optional)

Directions

1. Heat the oven to 325F. Set the baking dish with cooking spray.
2. In a mixing bowl, mix the cream cheese until smooth using an electric mixer. Add the powdered sugar and vanilla. Mix well.
3. Set the cream cheese mixture on the crepe, leaving 1/2-inch around the edge. Top with strawberries.
4. Roll up the crepe and place seam-side down in the prepared baking dish. Bake until lightly browned (about 10 minutes).
5. Cut the crepe in half. Transfer to two individual serving plates.

Nutrition:

Calories: 217	Carbs: 24g	Sodium: 177mg
Fat: 11g	Protein: 4g	Potassium: 89mg

207.   Apple-Berry Cobbler

Preparation time: 55 minutes   Cooking time: 40 minutes   Servings: 2

Ingredients:

The Filling:

- 1/3 cup fresh raspberries
- 1/3 cup fresh blueberries
- 2/3 cup chopped apples
- 2 tsp. turbinado or brown sugar
- 1/4 tsp. ground cinnamon
- 1/2 tsp. lemon zest
- 1 tsp. lemon juice
- 1/2 tbsp. cornstarch

The Topping:

- Egg white from 1/2 large egg
- 2 tbsp. soy milk
- 1/8 tsp. salt
- 1/4 tsp. vanilla
- 1/2 tbsp. turbinado or brown sugar
- 1/4 cup whole-wheat pastry flour

Directions:

1. Heat the oven to 350°F. Lightly coat two individual ovenproof ramekins with cooking spray.
2. In a medium bowl, combine raspberries, blueberries, apples, sugar, cinnamon, lemon zest, and lemon juice. Stir to mix evenly.
3. Add the cornstarch and stir until it dissolves. Set aside.
4. In a separate bowl, whisk the egg white until lightly beaten. Add the soy milk, salt, vanilla, sugar, and pastry flour. Stir to mix well.
5. Divide the fruit mixture evenly between the prepared ramekins. Spoon the topping over each. Place the ramekins on a large baking pan and put them in the oven.
6. Bake until the filling is tender and the topping is golden brown (about 30 minutes).

Nutrition:

Calories: 190	Carbs: 41g	Sodium: 150mg
Fat: 1g	Protein: 4g	Potassium: 191mg

208.   Vanilla Poached Peaches

Preparation time: 10 minutes   Cooking time: 30 minutes   Servings: 2

Ingredients:

- 1/2 cup water
- • 1/4 cup sugar
- • 1/2 vanilla bean, split and scraped
- • 2 large peaches, pitted and quartered

Directions:

1. Combine water, sugar, and vanilla bean in a saucepan. Over low heat, stir the mixture until the sugar dissolves. Continue to simmer until the mixture thickens (about 10 minutes).
2. Add the cut fruit. Simmer on low heat for about 5 minutes.

Nutrition:

Calories: 202	Carbs: 51g	Sodium: 1mg
Protein: 1.3g	Fat: 0.3g	Potassium: 285mg

209.   Mixed Berry Whole-Grain Cake

Preparation time: 15 minutes   Cooking time: 35 minutes   Servings: 2

Ingredients:

- 1/4 cup skim milk
- • 1/2 tbsp. vinegar
- • 1 tbsp. canola oil
- • 1/2 tsp. vanilla
- • 1/2 egg
- • 3 tbsp. packed brown sugar
- • 1/2 cup whole-wheat pastry flour
- • 1/2 cup frozen mixed berries

Directions:

1. Preheat the oven to 350F. Prepare a small cake pan with cooking spray and coat with flour.
2. In a bowl, mix milk, vinegar, oil, vanilla, egg, and brown sugar until smooth.
3. Stir in the flour just until moistened.
4. Carefully fold half the berries into the batter.
5. Spoon the mixture into the prepared pan. Sprinkle with the remaining berries.
6. Bake for 25 to 30 minutes or until golden brown and the top springs back when touched in the center.
7. Cool in the pan for 10 minutes.

Nutrition:

Calories: 307   Carbs: 55g   Sodium: 41mg

Fat: 7g   Protein: 6g   Potassium: 98mg

210.   Ambrosia with Coconut and Toasted Almonds

Preparation time: 15 minutes   Cooking time: 30 minutes   Servings: 2

Ingredients:

- 1/4 cup slivered almonds
- • 1/4 cup unsweetened shredded coconut
- • 1/2 small pineapple, cubed
- • 2 oranges, segmented
- • 1 red apple, cored and sliced
- • 1 tbsp. cream sherry

Directions:

1. Preheat the oven to 325F. Place almonds on a baking sheet and bake, stirring occasionally, until golden and fragrant, about 10 minutes. Transfer immediately to a plate to cool.
2. Add coconut to the sheet and bake, stirring often, until lightly browned, about 10 minutes. Transfer immediately to a plate to cool.
3. In a large bowl, combine pineapple, oranges, apples, and sherry. Stir gently to mix well.

Nutrition:

Calories: 386   Fat: 13g   Sodium: 20mg

Carbs: 68g   Protein: 5g   Potassium: 777mg

15.Index

16. Frequently Asked Questions (FAQs)

In this chapter, we will address common questions and misconceptions about the DASH diet to provide clarity and guidance for those considering adopting this healthy eating plan.

1. Is the DASH diet only for people with high blood pressure?

Although the DASH diet was initially developed to help individuals lower their blood pressure, it is a balanced and nutritious eating plan that can benefit anyone seeking to improve their overall health. The DASH diet emphasizes whole foods, fruits, vegetables, lean proteins, and healthy fats, making it an ideal choice for promoting heart health, managing weight, and preventing chronic diseases.

2. Will I lose weight on the DASH diet?

The DASH diet can aid in weight loss by promoting healthier food choices and portion control. While it is not specifically designed for weight loss, the emphasis on nutrient-dense, low-calorie foods can help create a calorie deficit, leading to weight loss over time.

3. Can I follow the DASH diet if I have diabetes?

Yes, the DASH diet is suitable for individuals with diabetes. The diet focuses on whole, unprocessed foods, high fiber intake, and low glycemic index foods, which can help manage blood sugar levels. However, it is essential to work closely with your healthcare provider or a registered dietitian to tailor the DASH diet to your specific needs.

4. Is the DASH diet suitable for vegetarians or vegans?

The DASH diet can be easily adapted to accommodate vegetarian or vegan preferences. While the standard DASH diet includes lean meats, poultry, and fish, plant-based protein sources such as legumes, tofu, tempeh, and seitan can be substituted to create a vegetarian or vegan-friendly version of the diet.

5. How long will it take to see results on the DASH diet?

The duration required to see results can vary depending on individual factors such as age, weight, and the severity of hypertension. Some people may notice improvements in their blood pressure within a few weeks, while others may take longer. It's important to be patient and consistent in following the DASH diet and incorporating other lifestyle changes, such as regular exercise and stress management, for optimal results.

6. Can I have cheat meals on the DASH diet?

The DASH diet is flexible and can accommodate occasional indulgences. It's important to maintain a balanced approach and focus on moderation when consuming foods high in sodium, saturated fats, or added sugars. Remember that long-term success on the DASH diet involves developing sustainable, healthy eating habits rather than adhering to a strict, restrictive regimen.

7. How can I manage sodium intake when dining out or eating processed foods?

When dining out, ask for dishes to be prepared without added salt, choose low-sodium options, and avoid high-sodium condiments such as soy sauce or salad dressings. When consuming processed foods, read nutrition labels carefully and select low-sodium or no-salt-added versions whenever possible.

By addressing these frequently asked questions, we hope to provide valuable insights into the DASH diet and its potential benefits for your health. The following chapters will offer a variety of delicious and nutritious DASH diet recipes to help you on your journey to better health.

17. Tracking Your Progress

In this chapter, we will discuss how to effectively monitor your blood pressure and other health markers, set realistic goals, and evaluate your progress while following the DASH diet. Tracking your progress is crucial in determining the success of your dietary changes and allows you to make any necessary adjustments.

Monitoring Blood Pressure

Regularly checking your blood pressure is essential when following the DASH diet. The primary goal of the DASH diet is to lower high blood pressure or prevent it from developing. To monitor your blood pressure:
a. Invest in a reliable home blood pressure monitor. This will enable you to check your blood pressure at any time and maintain a consistent record of your readings.
b. Follow proper measuring techniques. Sit quietly for a few minutes before taking your blood pressure, with your arm at heart level and both feet flat on the floor. Take two or three readings, a minute apart, and record the average.
c. Track your blood pressure regularly. Check your blood pressure at the same time each day, ideally in the morning and evening. Keep a log of your readings to share with your healthcare provider.

Monitoring Other Health Markers

In addition to blood pressure, it's essential to track other health markers, such as cholesterol levels, blood sugar levels, and body weight. Regular checkups with your healthcare provider will help you monitor these markers and ensure you stay on the right track.

Setting Realistic Goals

Setting achievable and specific goals is crucial for success. When following the DASH diet, focus on both short-term and long-term goals. For example:
a. Short-term goals: Increase fruit and vegetable intake to 5 servings per day, reduce sodium intake to under 2,300 mg per day, or incorporate 30 minutes of physical activity daily.
b. Long-term goals: Achieve a healthy body weight, maintain blood pressure within a healthy range, or improve overall cardiovascular health.

Evaluating Progress

Periodically evaluating your progress is essential to determine the effectiveness of the DASH diet and make any necessary adjustments. Consider the following steps:
a. Review your blood pressure log and other health markers. Compare your current readings to your initial baseline measurements and discuss any changes with your healthcare provider.
b. Assess your dietary habits. Review your food diary and ensure you're meeting the recommendations for daily servings of fruits, vegetables, whole grains, lean proteins, and low-fat dairy.
c. Reflect on your goals. Evaluate your progress toward your short-term and long-term goals. Celebrate your achievements and adjust your goals as needed.
d. Seek support. Share your progress with friends, family, or a support group. They can offer encouragement, advice, and motivation to help you stay on track.

By consistently monitoring your blood pressure and other health markers, setting realistic goals, and evaluating your progress, you can maximize the benefits of the DASH diet and improve your overall health.

18.BONUS: VIDEO LECTURES

The Dash diet can provide useful benefit for people suffering of HBP, reducing dependance on drugs. So, we thought that you would appreciate having 15 video lectures to consult to furtherly clarify some of the concepts discussed in this book.

You can find them at this link:

Video Lecture Link

Conclusion

Many people do not realize how much salt they consume in their regular diet. It is straightforward to go over your daily sodium allowance when eating at fast-food restaurants because the food often has a lot of salt. By eating at restaurants and not controlling your sodium intake, you could easily consume 3 or 4 times your daily salt limit. By switching to a dash diet, you can still go out to eat at restaurants and manage your salt consumption. The DASH diet will allow you to control your sodium consumption while allowing fast food at restaurants that may not have lower sodium choices.

The dash diet is a precise way to lose weight and lower blood pressure without spending hours cooking exotic recipes. This diet is also a great way to stay healthy. If you try to stick to the diet's prescribed foods, you can lose weight, lower your blood pressure, and lower your threat of heart disease. This diet is easy to follow and can be followed by anyone. It does not require a lot of time to shop for food or cook the food, making it easy for you to follow.

The dash diet is also very well suited to work with any lifestyle. If you have kids, you can ensure that they follow the proper portion sizes of the foods on the dash diet, so they will not overeat and gain weight. When you have high blood pressure, you must start eating right and reduce it. The dash diet is the precise way to do this. The dash diet does not demand you to be religious about what you eat, but it encourages heart-healthy foods such as fruits, vegetables, whole grains, and nuts. This cookbook is a way for you to lower your blood pressure quickly. By following these easy steps, you will reduce your blood pressure and increase the quality of your life.

If you enjoyed this book, we would really appreciate a review:
Review Link

Made in the USA
Las Vegas, NV
09 June 2024